OUR BLOOD RELATIONS;

OR, THE

DARWINIAN THEORY.

OUR BLOOD RELATIONS;

OR, THE

DARWINIAN THEORY.

"So grossly ignorant are many of us of our blood relations."—
Review of DESCENT OF MAN, '*Times*,' *April 8th*, 1871.

ASCIDI, *Linnæus.* "THEYTON OF THE ANCIENTS," *Cuvier.*

"Man's most ancient progenitor apparently consisted of a group of marine animals resembling the larvæ of existing Ascidians."— DESCENT OF MAN.

LONDON: SIMPKIN, MARSHALL, & Co.

BATH: R. E. PEACH, 8, BRIDGE STREET.

1872.

BATH :

R. E. PEACH, BRIDGE STREET.

PREFACE.

WE are perfectly aware how difficult it is to treat the doctrine of the "Darwinian theory," as it ought to be treated, in the very limited space of such a work as this; but the issue at stake is so momentous, the result of a general adherence to the principles laid down, and the conclusions arrived at in the 'Descent of Man' would be so ruinous to our religious and social feelings and institutions, that the Author is induced to hope that an exposition of them in a popular style, and in a small compass, may be of some use, if not, as successfully combating the peculiar views expounded by Mr. Darwin, at least as tending to draw renewed attention to his works, and to the necessity of unhesitatingly exposing the fallacy, even in a scientific point of view, of conclusions which contemptuously ignore all revealed religion, and all faith in our Bible as the inspired Word of God.

If Mr. Darwin's book were an ephemeral publication, which, with the effect it at first produced, would soon pass away and be replaced by some other topic of literary interest, it might be better so to allow it to sink into oblivion. But as the work of one of the most distinguished naturalists of the age, as containing views highly in accordance with a growing spirit of irrational philosophy and materialism, it has become and will remain as a standard book in our scientific literature, and one calculated to effect more harm than we dare think of, if its apparently unintentional but poisonous influences are not neutralised by some antidote.

In the "Introduction" will be found a brief abstract of the Darwinian theory, with the inevitable consequences to which it leads; and the "Notes" supply fuller explanation on various points than could be given in the text, together with references to the pages of the 'Descent of Man,' from which the extracts are taken, and to the opinions of other authors and writers. The writer of the following pages does not wish to assert or even to imply that Mr. Darwin, by his publication of the 'Descent of Man' had any avowed or unexpressed intention of making an attack upon what is by some called religion; but wishes to state plainly and unhesitatingly that, if the conclusions arrived at in that book are admitted, particularly as regards the creation of man, we must not only renounce all belief in the Scripture narrative of Creation, but must also give up our belief in the doctrine of original sin and of the Atonement, of the Sabbath as a Divine ordinance, of our duty to our God, our faith as Christians, and, in fact, fall back to the state, or even to a lower state, of morality and religious belief than in the days of the heathen philosophers.

January, 1872.

INTRODUCTION.

WITH a view of assisting those who have neither leisure nor inclination to wade through Mr. Darwin's books, and yet who ought to know the results that would follow the general acceptance of the conclusions at which he has arrived, we will endeavour to give a brief abstract of what is called the " Darwinian Theory " as expounded in his 'Origin of Species' and the 'Descent of Man.'

This theory mainly depends on the Doctrine of Evolution, or the gradual development during an un-limited period of time of animal life from one species into a different species, or different group, until, by insensible graduation, a simple monad may be ulti-mately evolved into *Man*.

The two principal agents employed by Mr. Darwin to produce such wonderful results are " Natural Selec-tion " and " Sexual Selection," which are thus defined by him :—" Sexual selection depends on the success of certain individuals over others of the same sex in re-lation to the propagation of the species ; whilst natural selection depends upon the success of both sexes, at all ages, in relation to the general conditions of life."— *Descent of Man*, vol. ii. p. 398.

The results of the action of these agents are thus described in the 'Descent of Man.' There now exists a class or sub-order of marine Molluscs called Ascidians, which are " invertebrate, hermaphrodite, marine crea-tures permanently attached to a support. They hardly appear like animals, and consist of a simple, tough, leathery sack, with two small projecting orifices;" "their larvæ somewhat resemble tadpoles in shape, and have the power of swimming freely about." Some foreign naturalists have recently discovered, or fancy they have discovered, that " the larvæ of Ascidians are related to the Vertebrata, in their manner of development, in the relative positions of the nervous system, and in possessing a structure closely like the *chorda dorsalis* of vertebrate animals." By this "discovery of extraordinary interest," "we have," says Mr. Darwin, " at last gained a clue to the source whence the Vertebrata have been derived. *We should thus be justified in believing* that at an extremely remote period a group of animals existed, resembling in many respects the larvæ of our present Ascidians, *which diverged into two great branches*—the one *retrograding* in development and producing the present class of Ascidians, the other rising to *the crown and summit* of the animal kingdom " (that is to Man) " by giving birth to the Vertebrata." —*Descent of Man*, vol. i. pp. 205-206.

Having thus by an extraordinary effort of imagination found the key to the kingdom of the Vertebrata, the clue is eagerly followed up, and is thus easily disposed of:—" The most ancient progenitors in the kingdom of the Vertebrata, at which we are able to obtain an *obscure glance, apparently* consisted of a class of marine animals, resembling the larvæ of existing Ascidians. These animals *probably* gave rise to a group of fishes. . . . From such fish a *very small advance would* carry us on to the amphibians." . . . "Birds and reptiles were more intimately connected together." . . . "*But no one can at present say* by what line of descent the three higher and related classes, namely, mammals, birds, and reptiles, were derived from either of the other two lower vertebrate classes, namely, amphibians and fishes. In the class of mammals the steps *are not difficult* to conceive which led from the lowest in the class up to the Old and New World monkeys—and from the latter, at a remote period, Man, the wonder and glory of the universe, proceeded." —*Descent of Man*, vol. i. pp. 212-213.

"Thus," says Mr. Darwin, "we have given to Man a pedigree of prodigious length, but not, it may be said, of noble quality."—*Ibid.*

And to prevent any possible misconception of the results of this mode of succession, Mr. Darwin says:— "The belief that animals so distinct as a monkey or elephant and a humming-bird, a snake, frog, and fish, &c., could all have sprung from the *same parents, will appear monstrous* to those who have not attended to the recent progress of natural history. For this belief implies the former *existence* of links closely binding together all these forms, now so utterly unlike."—Vol. i. p. 203. Monstrous indeed—if the progress in science had not been equalled by the progress in the credulity of some scientific men. The means by which these extraordinary results have been obtained are, as above mentioned, by the agencies of "Natural selection" and "Sexual selection." "Natural selection" is called the "survival of the fittest," that is, that all animals increase in number more rapidly than their means of subsistence increases; that many must die before the usual term of animal life, either by epidemic disease, by famine or drought, by the ravages of other animals, such as the destruction of herbivorous animals by the carnivora, and by fighting with those of their own species, &c. In all these cases the weakest, the least active, the infirm in any way, would be the first to succumb: the strong, the active, the most healthy would survive, and it would be by these that the various races would be kept up; and it is a maxim of this theory that this struggle for existence would cause certain developments of a superior class to necessarily appear, which would give superiority to their possessors, and which, being inherited by their offspring, would, granted an unlimited period of time, insensibly progress from species to species and groups, or "that a humming-bird and an elephant" would proceed from the same parental stock.

But as this theory does not account for all the facts required for the complete development of the system, Mr. Darwin in his 'Descent of Man' has added another, that of "Sexual selection," or the influence of the sensual and sexual passions upon the progress of animal life. It is discovered that, although the males are the wooers, and the most ardent in the gratification of their passions, as a rule, so many males are at the same time desirous of possessing any one female, that these latter have the power of selection, which they exert to a great extent; and as it is supposed to be natural that the females should select the strongest, the handsomest, the most perfect—and as the males exert all their arts in showing themselves off to the best advantage—it is contended that the breed being thus carried on by the most perfect, and by the *desire* of the males to become more perfect and attractive, slight modifications or improvements in form, &c., would naturally occur, which, as in the case of natural selection, would *in an unlimited* time produce, in conjunction with the other causes, all the necessary changes from the humming-bird to the elephant.

We believe the above to be a fair though very condensed view of the Darwinian theory, which, had it been put forward as a suggestion for the consideration of the scientific world and of theologians, might have been treated as an ingenious, speculative, though mischievous, theory; but, so far from this being the case, it is advanced with all the dogmatism of a demonstrated problem, with such expressions as these:—" Unless we *wilfully close our eyes* we may, with our present knowledge, approximately recognise our parentage;" "It is *incredible* that all these facts should speak falsely;" "He who is not content to *look like a savage*, at the phenomena of nature as disconnected, *cannot any longer believe* that *man* is the work of a *separate creation*;" "The grounds upon which this conclusion rests will never be shaken;" "The great principle of Evolution stands up clear and firm;" "It is only our natural prejudice, and that arrogance which made our forefathers declare that they were descended from demigods, which leads us to demur to this conclusion;" "And to take any other view of man's origin is to admit that our structure and that of all the animals around us is a *mere* snare laid to entrap our judgment;" "On any other view" (than that of descent from a common progenitor) "the similarity of pattern between the hand of a man or monkey, the foot of a horse, the flapper of a seal, the wing of a bat, &c., is *utterly inexplicable*. It is no *scientific* explanation to assert that they have all been formed on the same ideal plan;" "No other explanation has ever been given of the *marvellous* fact, that the embryo of a man, dog, seal, bat, reptile, &c., can at first be hardly distinguished from each other;" "But the time will before long come when it will be thought wonderful that *naturalists* should believe that each animal was the work of a separate act of creation."—*Descent of Man.*

The above quotations are sufficient to show the confidence with which Mr. Darwin has arrived at his conclusions.

The direct pedigree and immediate *birth of man* is thus described:—"We may infer that some ancient member of the anthropomorphous sub-group" (of apes, such as the gorilla, chimpanzee, orang) *"gave birth to man."*—Vol. i. p. 197. "We do not know whether man is descended from some comparatively small species like the chimpanzee, or from one as powerful as the gorilla;" and "We thus learn that man is descended from a hairy quadruped, furnished with a tail and pointed ears, *probably* arboreal in its habits, and an inhabitant of the Old World." "It is somewhat more probable that our early progenitors lived on the African continent than elsewhere."—Vol. i. p. 199.

But although the *birth* of man is thus known, it would, says Mr. Darwin, "be impossible to fix on any definite point *when* the *term* Man ought to be used. *But this is a matter of very little importance.*"—Vol. i. p. 235.

Mr. Darwin also contends that the present man is descended from Barbarians. He says "that to believe that man was aboriginally civilised, and then suffered utter degradation in so many regions, is to take a pitiably low view of human nature."—*Descent of Man,* vol. i. p. 184.

We have thus endeavoured to give, in as few words as possible, a general idea of the Darwinian theory. The first impulse on reading it must be its total contradiction to the Scripture narrative of the Creation. But Mr. Darwin thus combats the idea that there can be anything irreligious in the conclusions he has arrived at:—"I am aware that the conclusions arrived at in this work will be denounced by some as highly irreligious; but he who thus denounces them is bound to show why it is more irreligious to explain the origin of man as a distinct species by descent from some lower

form, through the laws of variation and natural se-
lection, than to explain the birth of the individual
through the laws of ordinary reproduction."—Vol. ii.
p. 395.

And, as regards the immortality of the soul, Mr.
Darwin summarily disposes of any consideration of that
point in these words:—" Few persons feel any anxiety
from the impossibility of determining at what precise
period in the development of the individual, from the
first trace of the minute germinal vesicle to the child
either before or after birth, man becomes an immortal
being; and there is no greater cause for anxiety, be-
cause the period in the ascending organic scale cannot
possibly be determined."—*Ibid.*

So that the fact *when* a certain animal became man,
and *when* that man was endowed with an immortal
soul, appears to be of little moment in a work pur-
porting to give a scientific account of the "Descent of
Man."

The object of the following pages is to show the
fallacy of the conclusions thus arrived at, even in a
scientific point of view, and that this Darwinian theory
cannot be accepted without a perfect disbelief in the
Bible as the revealed Word of God, on evidence
the most incomplete and unsatisfactory; also that all,
or the greater portion of the *facts* detailed in proof of
" natural selection " and " sexual selection " may be
admitted, but the conclusions derived from these facts
denied : as, so far from proving that one group of animals
ever merged into a group of different form and struc-
ture, they merely show that, as all animals were created
perfect at first, it was necessary that the "fittest"
should survive to preserve the races in their original
perfect state, as otherwise they must have degenerated
and the same holds good with " sexual selection." To

preserve all animal life from deteriorating, it was necessary that the most perfect of the various races should cohabit, so as to continue the breed in its original state of perfectness; and animals were endowed with their sensual and sexual instincts in order that the original state of the various classes might be preserved. But that either of these agents could change animals from their original nature, or produce a humming-bird and an elephant from the same parentage, there is no evidence whatever to show. We know that certain variations "in species" may take place to meet altered conditions of life, climate, &c., both in animals and in plants; but we know also, that there is a *limit* to these variations, beyond which they cannot pass; and that there is no *evidence* either of extinct or of any living species having passed these limits.

Cuvier, in his Introduction to his 'Règne Animal,' says, "that the abundance and species of nutriment, with other causes, exercise great influence, and this influence may extend to the whole body in general, or to certain organs in particular; thence arises the impossibility of a perfect similitude between the offspring and parent. Differences of this kind in organised beings, form what are called *varieties*." Again he says :—

" There is no proof that all the differences which now distinguish organised beings are such as may have been produced by circumstances. All that has been advanced upon this subject is hypothetical. Experience, on the contrary, appears to prove that, in the actual state of the globe, *varieties are confined within rather narrow limits*, and, go back as far as we may, we shall still find these limits the same."

We are quite aware that we shall be told that Cuvier is out of date, that his time is gone by,—" Nous avons changé tout cela," say our modern naturalists; but before we give up the father of comparative anatomy, we must have something more, in the shape of precise science, than the conjectures and imaginary speculations of the Darwinian theory, which is founded on the supposition that because certain *varieties* can be observed in the same species of animals, therefore as these varieties have occurred in a certain time, given an unlimited time during which these varieties would continue to increase, the first little atom of change would, step by step, advance in a kind of geometrical progression, until the whole nature of the animal became changed, and the same parentage gave rise to a humming-bird and to an elephant, to a tadpole and to a man.

But this ignores entirely the principle of the limitations of varieties laid down by Cuvier, and even now accepted by many distinguished naturalists.

Professor Huxley, an ardent supporter of the theory of evolution, admits in one of his essays published in 1870 (see 'Times' of April 8, 1871), "that it is not absolutely proven that a group of animals, having all the characteristics exhibited by a group in nature, has ever been originated by selection, whether artificial or natural." "Groups having the morphological character of species, distinct and permanent races, in fact, have been so produced over and over again; but there is no positive evidence, at present, that any group of animals has, by *variation* and selective breeding, given rise to another group which was *even in the least degree infertile* with the first; but still, as the case stands at present, this little rift within the lute is not to be disguised or overlooked."

But as we know that animals within a certain degree of affinity are *infertile* with each other, "*this little rift within the lute*" is, as remarked by the critic in the 'Times,' "more than sufficient to spoil the music." And yet it is with the inharmonious sounds produced by this cracked instrument that the author of the 'Descent of Man' would seek to replace the perfect harmony of the laws of Nature, and of the scheme of Creation as revealed to us in God's Word.

Nothing can show the extent to which Mr. Darwin carries his views, and his utter contempt for any knowledge but that of human reason, than the following remarkable passage :—" But it is a hopeless endeavour to decide this point on sound grounds, until some definition of the term 'species' is generally accepted ; and the definition *must not* include an element which *cannot possibly be ascertained*, such as an *act of creation*." Vol. i. p. 228.—This one passage is sufficient to stamp the character of Mr. Darwin's views.

Mr. Darwin says those who denounce his conclusions as irreligious are bound to show " why it is more irreligious to explain the origin of Man as a distinct species by descent from some lower form, through the process of variation and natural selection, than to explain the birth of the individual through the laws of ordinary reproduction. The birth both of the species and of the individual are equally parts of that grand sequence of events which our minds refuse to accept as *the results of blind chance*."—Vol. ii. p. 396.

It depends a good deal upon what Mr. Darwin means by " irreligious." If he applies it to heathens, to the Infidels of China, to the Hindoos of India, or to a mere believer in some creative power, we will not argue the case with him ; but if by it he means anything contrary to revealed religion as accepted and understood by those who profess what is called Christianity, then we say most decidedly that his conclusions are highly irreligious, as they contain a direct attack on, or rather a total ignoring of, the scheme of Creation as revealed to us in the Bible.

To accept Mr. Darwin's views, we must not only ignore the account of the Creation, of all life, and of Man, as given in the Bible, but also the whole account of what occurred to Man immediately after the Creation, as given in the four subsequent chapters, as also all references made to this narrative in other parts of the Bible. The New Testament then necessarily follows, and with it Christianity and our knowledge of our Saviour, the doctrine of original sin, and of the Atonement, &c. We must also give up the Sabbath as a Divine institution, as this seventh day of rest is founded on the act of Creation. As a merely social institution, it has not been found necessary by the hundreds of millions in China, in India, in all Asia and Africa. Take away its Divine command, make it a mere secular ordinance, and it will become a record of the past in our own country. To accept Mr. Darwin's conclusions, we must renounce our faith, and revert to the Greek and Roman philosophy, if indeed we could now, deprived of the influence of revealed religion, retain even the practical virtues of that philosophy.

It is not for Christians to show cause why all animal life could not as well have arrived at its present state by gradual development as by distinct acts of creation. We have God's revealed Word that Man was separately created, and we maintain that everything in Nature agrees with that account, and that nothing has been discovered to shake our faith in that great fact; and therefore it rests with those who do not believe in Man's creation, as revealed in God's Word, to show that our belief is ill-founded, and to give most convincing reasons for their conclusions.

B

And what are we offered in exchange for this renunciation of our faith? A system founded on mere conjecture, in the first place in supposing that a certain group of animals existed, of which nothing is known; then we are to suppose that these imaginary animals gave birth to certain offspring, who diverged into *two* different branches, contrary to the fundamental law of Nature, " that every organised being reproduces others that are similar to itself, otherwise death, being a necessary consequence of life, the *species* would soon become extinct" (*Cuvier's* 'Natural History'); then that one of these branches *retrograded,* contrary to the first principle of evolution, which is progress; that the other branch, by some unknown cause, developed into the crown and summit of the animal kingdom. Having thus invented an imaginary germ of vertebrate life, the remaining solution of the problem appears to Mr. Darwin to be easy and simple. We are asked to believe that these vertebrates *probably* became fishes; then a very *small advance*—how effected is left to the imagination—would carry us to the amphibians; "*but no one can at present say* how these amphibians became reptiles, birds, and mammals." " In mammals the steps are *not difficult to conceive,*" &c. " *We may then ascend* to the Lemuridæ, and the *interval is not wide* to other classes," &c.

Is all this imagination—is all this conjecture—science? are " apparently " " probably " scientific terms? Is the introduction of an imaginary group of animals, as the basis of all animated nature, a scientific mode of reasoning?

We are told that if any single link in this chain of succession had never existed, " Man would not have been exactly what he now is." And we are also told :—
" But no one can at present say by what line of descent

the three higher and related classes, namely, mammals, birds, and reptiles, were derived from either of the two lower vertebrate classes, namely, amphibians and fishes." Yet with this fragment of a chain, the absence of a single link of which would be fatal to our being now what we are, we are told that, unless we "wilfully close our eyes," or "are content to look like a savage," &c. &c., we *must* admit the conclusions founded on such pitiful evidence; and that, on any other grounds, certain known facts in Natural History are utterly unintelligible and inexplicable. Are we to renounce our faith on such evidence as this? Of course we are aware that as "all things are possible with God," there is nothing opposed to God's *Omnipotence* in saying that animals and Man were produced in accordance with any imaginable theory; but we say that we have God's revealed Word, that the creation of the world and all that is therein was effected in a particular manner, and we believe that this account is consistent with all our researches into the laws and workings of Nature, and that nothing can be produced to show that it is not so, and therefore that the onus of showing the contrary rests with our opponents. It would clearly be utterly impossible in such a work as this to allude even to the various arguments contained in the 'Descent of Man,' but we may select one or two, as illustrative of the different conclusions to be drawn from the same facts.

Take the case of the ornamentations on the caterpillar. Mr. Darwin says, " It occurred to me that some caterpillars were splendidly coloured, and as sexual selection could not possibly have acted, it appeared rash to attribute the beauty of the mature insect to this agency, unless the bright colour of their larvæ (which do not stand in any close correlation to those of the mature insect) could be in some manner ex-

B 2

plained, as their bright colours do not serve in any ordinary manner as a protection."—Vol. i. p. 415. A suggestion was made by Mr. A. R. Wallace, that probably these caterpillars had " distastefulness " given to them as a protection, and that their bright colours served to point them out to birds, &c., that they were unfit for food.   Mr. J. Jenner Weir found that the birds in his aviary would not touch this class of caterpillar; and Mr. A. Butler gave them to some lizards and frogs, by whom they were rejected. " Thus," says Mr. Darwin, " the probable truth of Mr. Wallace's view is confirmed, namely, that certain caterpillars have been made conspicuous for their own good, so as to be easily recognised by their enemies."   " This view will, it is probable, be hereafter extended to many animals which are coloured in a conspicuous manner."—Vol. i. p. 417.

As Mr. Darwin says that it *appeared rash* to attribute this beautiful colouring of caterpillars to sexual selection, *unless* it could be in some manner explained, we presume that, as it has been so explained to his satisfaction, he does now attribute it to " sexual selection."

And that he does so attribute it, is evidently inferred by Mr. A. R. Wallace, who says in his review of the 'Descent of Man,' in the 'Academy' of March 15, 1871, "Coleoptera are almost all palpably protected, either by resembling inanimate objects, by obscurity, by hard coats of mail, or by being distasteful to birds; and those of the two latter categories are almost all conspicuously coloured. It seems to me more probable, therefore, that the colours of insects are due to *the same unknown laws* which have produced the colours of caterpillars, than that they are due to sexual selection. In caterpillars we have almost all the classes of coloration found in perfect insects. We have protective and conspicuous tints; and among the latter we have spots, streaks, bands, and patterns, perfectly definite in character, and of the most brilliantly contrasted hues. We have also many ornamental appendages; beautiful fleshy tubercles or tentacles, hard spines, beautifully coloured hairs arranged in tufts, brushes, starry clusters, or long pencils, and horns on the head and tail, either single or double, pointed or clubbed. Now if all these beautiful and varied ornaments can be produced and rendered constant in each species, by *some unknown cause* quite independent of sexual selection, why cannot the *same cause* produce the colours and many of the ornaments of perfect insects, subjected as they are to so much greater variety of conditions than their larvæ?" And Mr. Wallace, in the concluding lines of his paper, leaves no doubt as to what he means by " these unknown causes, or laws."

This account of the caterpillar is full of instruction, and seems to break down the theory of sexual selection in butterflies, if not in all insects; and as Mr. Darwin remarks that, " this view will, it is probable, be extended to many animals which are coloured in a conspicuous manner," it strikes an equally hard blow at the general principle of sexual selection, and indeed of "natural selection;" for if some unknown cause produced these beautiful colours and ornamentation in so evanescent a creature as a caterpillar, why not in birds and animals?

No doubt these larvæ, which are the food of birds and reptiles, must be protected in some manner, or they and the insects arising from them would soon cease to exist. Some so resemble the leaves and twigs of trees, that they can scarcely be distinguished from them. Others, which are very conspicuous, are distasteful, and their very conspicuousness saves them from certain of their enemies, but not from all, as, if they were uniformly distasteful, so as not to be the food of anything else, they would so multiply as to overrun and destroy everything. When we see that the wasp puts a small grub or caterpillar into every cell with the egg, we may imagine the myriads destroyed in this one manner; and no doubt this ornamental caterpillar has its enemies, though we may not precisely know what they are: the beautiful balance of Nature is always kept up, but not by natural or sexual selection, not by the whim or caprice of individuals, but by a far higher cause, and by far higher though to us unknown laws. From the smallest insect to the largest beast, all have their enemies, all are kept down to their proper numerical position in the scale of life, by some mysterious but never varying laws; and all that is here attributed to natural and sexual selection is merely some of the means for continuing the various races in their state of original perfectness, and for keeping them within the limits assigned to them by unerring wisdom and design in the first scheme of Creation. But the wonderful beauty and variety of ornament in the caterpillar, described by Mr. Wallace, was not required merely to make the larvæ conspicuous. Mr. Darwin quotes Mr. Bates's description of a large caterpillar in South America, about four inches in length, transversely banded with black and yellow (similar to a German sentry-box), and with its head, legs, and tail of a bright red, visible to the eye of a man or of a bird at many yards" (vol. i. p. 416).

Nothing but distastefulness could save this caterpillar from destruction, except by some particular bird or reptile, whose allotted food it is, so as to keep it down to its proper position in the scale of life; but in this case no great beauty is required to make it conspicuous, none of the exquisite ornamentation described by Mr. Wallace.

Apply the same principle to snakes, as highly ornamented as any class of created forms. Some venomous, and some harmless snakes, the beautifully coloured coral-snakes of South America, inhabit the same districts, and are so like each other that "no one but a naturalist could distinguish the harmless from the poisonous kinds." Mr. Wallace "believes that the innocuous kinds have acquired their similarity of appearance and colour to the venomous kind as a protection, as they would naturally be thought dangerous by their enemies" (vol. ii. p. 31). How the innocuous snakes came to know that others, just like them were venomous, we are not told. Mr. Darwin thinks the bright colours of the venomous classes may *perhaps* be due to sexual selection (vol. i. p. 32), but it is not shown that female snakes prefer bright coloured ones; and it is said to be very doubtful whether the bright colours of snakes serve them as any protection—the green tints of tree-snakes, &c., serve them, not so much for protection as to conceal them from *their prey.*

But as regards birds, the case of the caterpillar is still stronger. Could any description give a more accurate account of the beauty of the plumage of birds, than that given by Mr. Wallace of caterpillars:—"Spots, streaks, bands, and patterns, of the most brilliantly contrasted hues, beautiful fleshy tubercles or tentacles; hard spines, beautifully coloured hairs arranged in tufts, brushes, starry clusters, or long pencils; horns on the head and tail, either single or double"? Could any words more exactly describe the varied plumage and ornamentation of birds? and if all this beautiful ornamentation (for the plain black and yellow bands of the South American caterpillar would have equally answered every purpose of conspicuousness) is due to an unknown cause, and given for some other purpose than mere utility, have we not a right to infer that the beautiful plumage of birds and colours of some animals were given to them not merely for the purposes of natural and sexual selection, but by the same beneficent Being who clothed the lilies of the field, and made all nature, animate and inanimate, both beautiful and useful to the Man whom He created to rule over them?

Following up this inquiry, we come to that of the Argus Pheasant, on which Mr. Darwin bestows ten pages of description and illustration, to prove that the ocelli or peculiar markings on the wing-feathers of this beautiful bird were produced gradually by "sexual selection," or by the desire to attract the female, and not created as we now see them; and says, "No one, I presume, will attribute the shading, which has excited the admiration of many experienced artists, to *chance*— to the fortuitous concourse of atoms of colouring matter. Because this beautiful ball-and-socket shading on the chief wing-feathers, is more perfect, and better defined, than are the secondary wing-feathers, which have only the first trace of an ocellus, and thus prove to demonstration that a graduation is at least possible, from a mere spot to a finished ball-and-socket ocellus;" and thus concludes his account of the plumage of this bird :— "As the secondary plumes became lengthened through *sexual selection,* and as the elliptic ornaments increased in diameter, their colours apparently became *less bright ;* and then the ornamentation of the plumes, having degenerated, had to be gained by improvements in the pattern and shading; and this process has been carried on, until the wonderful ball-and-socket ocelli have been finally developed. Thus we can understand—and *in no other way* as it seems to me—the present condition and origin of the ornaments on the wing-feathers of the Argus Pheasant " (vol. ii. pp. 141–151).

As we are told that the female birds prefer the more attractive males, and it is by desiring to be attractive that these beautiful ball-and-socket ocelli have been gradually formed from a simple dark spot on the inner wing-feathers, through various stages, to the *elliptic* ornaments, and *from them* to the circular ball-and-socket ocelli, how came it that some to whom these feathers have been shown in their various stages, think the elliptic spots *even more beautiful* than the ball-and-socket ocelli? We can only suppose that the female Argus Pheasant has a different idea of beauty from these naturalists. It would appear to be Mr. Darwin's feeling that everything that cannot be scientifically accounted for, *must* be the result of *mere chance*. " I presume that no one will attribute the shading on the wing of an Argus Pheasant to *chance*." He says, " The mind refuses to accept the grand sequence of events " (as detailed in the scheme of evolution) " as *blind chance*." Can he not, or will he not allow, that those *unknown laws* which Mr. Wallace says he admits, have been the real cause of all these beautiful and beneficent arrangements, which he attributes to *blind chance?* If Mr. Darwin cannot do this, and for "chance" insert "design," we can ; and we refer him to the unswerving laws of Nature, as created and controlled by an omnipotent and beneficent God, for the true explanation of the facts regarding sexual selection, to which he has devoted five hundred pages of his 'Descent of Man.' But, curiously enough, he admits, in his 'Origin of Species,' that the preservation of even highly beneficial variations would depend to a certain extent on *chance* (vol. ii. p. 125).

But what does this examination of the wing-feathers of this beautiful bird show? Simply this, that on the short secondary wing-feathers *nearest* to the body there are irregular rows of spots; that on the succeeding wing-feathers those spots become developed into an elliptic ornament or spot, which again increases in its shorter diameter, and appears as a perfect circle or ocellus or ball-and-socket spot in the largest or most conspicuous secondary feathers; but it is noticeable that in the wing-feathers *farthest* from the body these ocelli are smaller and less perfect than on the other feathers; and as the uppermost ocellus in the longer secondary feathers appears to have the upper part sliced off, that is, the circle is not quite perfect; Mr. Darwin says, "it would, I think, perplex any one who believes that the plumage of the Argus pheasant was created as we now see it, to account for the imperfect condition of the uppermost ocelli" (vol. ii. p. 148).

All that we see here is, that the markings on the socondary wing-feathers of an Argus pheasant consist of a series of ornamental spots more or less developed according to their position in the wing,—the longer feathers having their spots in the greatest perfection, the feathers nearest the body having the spots smaller, forming, in fact, a gradual gradation or shadowing, making a most harmonious whole; but there is nothing whatever to show that the perfect ocellus on the long wing-feathers was ever the mere spot such as those on the feathers nearest the body, or that they have been in any way changed by natural selection, or even, supposing another million or so of years of this progress should go on, so as to make all the spots on all the feathers the same as the perfect ocellus, that the wing would be at all *more beautiful* or more attractive to the female. We believe the gradual gradation and shading of the spots as *they now are* and *always have been*, to be more beautiful than any alteration could make them. The whole description of these feathers is only another proof of the power, wisdom, and goodness of the Being who created this beautiful bird.

When Mr. Darwin says that on any other view (than that of descent from a common progenitor) the similarity of pattern between the hand of a man or monkey, the foot of a horse, the flapper of a seal, the wing of a bat, &c., *is utterly inexplicable,* the reply is that, as *one fundamental principle* pervades the structure of all animal life, it is to be expected that a certain similarity should exist between those portions of the anatomy of different animals as are intended to perform the same purposes, though differing in form and action in each class. Such similarity is perfectly consistent with the harmony of nature's laws.

And again, when Mr. Darwin says *that no other explanation* can be given of the marvellous fact that the embryo of a man, dog, seal, bat, reptile, &c., can at first hardly be distinguished from each other, we reply, as before, that as man in his physical structure resembles animals, and as all animals were created on one grand principle, we have, as it were, one fundamental form of existence; that these similarities in their embryonic development are again but one more proof of the wonderful harmony in the scheme of Creation, and do not (unless seen through the distorted medium of the most powerful evolution spectacles) afford the slightest *proof* that these various animals gradually developed one from the other.

We have in this Introduction confined ourselves to the creation of man in his physical structure, as having been developed from the lowest forms of animal life: the still more important point of Man's Mind, his moral sense and conscience, &c., having been equally developed from animals, will be discussed in the Text and in the Notes.

"OUR BLOOD RELATIONS."

"So grossly ignorant are many of us of our blood relations."
Review of DESCENT OF MAN, 'Times,' *April* 8, 1871.

PART I.

"NATURE and Nature's laws lay hid in Night,
God said, 'Let Newton be,' and all was Light."

Thus sang the Poet, in whose simple Faith
Almighty Power centred in " He saith ;"
But now, alas! too many faith deride,
And trust to Reason as their only guide.

"That God created man " has been believed,
Throughout all time, and as a truth received
Beyond all thought of question or dispute,
Which none till now have ventured to refute.
That man was made at once, as he is now,
Is the belief we fearlessly avow.
But certain naturalists now profess,
By means of *Modern Science,* to possess
To " Man's Descent " the long-desired key,
By which to solve that mighty mystery—
And now presume, misled by learning's pride,
How Man was first engendered, to decide.
And step by step, and link by link, to trace
His upward progress to the human race ;
To let no tittle of the clue escape,
From the first monad to the hirsute Ape,

The Ape as Man's true ancestor they claim,*
Denying that from God direct he came.

Reject all truths their wisdom cannot sound,
Set faith aside, on Reason take their ground—
Whilst Nature's works in ev'rything display
Unerring Wisdom and Design, they say
All creatures were, as chance or fancy led,
By evolution, or selection, bred
From one sole source, from which, as Time revolved,
All species and all races were evolved.

This is the order, these the means, and ends,
On which this monad theory depends.

The larva of a mollusc,† we are told,
Progressed into a fish; the fish made bold
Th' amphibian's form to take, which was transferred,
Through various grades of reptiles, to a bird.
This was Love's holiday; ‡ the hills and dales
Were resonant with music, and the vales
With sweetest melody; the woodlands rung
With joyous carols, as the warblers sung
Their little love-tales with harmonious voice,
Each to the pretty partner of his choice.

The bigger birds, in brilliant hues arrayed,
Their gorgeous plumage artfully displayed: §
With feats grotesque, and postures strange, they thought
The favour of their charmers could be bought;
Who watched their antics with a critic's eye,
And goaded them to fiercest rivalry.

---

* See Introduction, p. 9. † Ibid. p. 8.
‡ 'Descent of Man,' vol. ii. pp. 38–238. § See Note I.—Page 44.

A happy time !—no wonder that the sage
With keenest relish lingers on its page.

This constant emulation bore its fruits,*
And birds assumed the structure of the brutes:
Then love grew coarser, fiercer grew the fights,
Brute force alone decided lovers' rights.
Race after race continually progressed,
And higher forms and attributes possessed,—
Ever improving, spreading o'er the earth,
As time rolled on, an Ape to Man gave birth.
Thus Man, the pride and glory of his race,
Back to a tadpole can his lineage trace.

Unless in wilful blindness,† we must see
And candidly admit our pedigree.
"Our blood relations" of the leath'ry sack,
If not too noble, date a long time back—
To meet the wondrous changes thus produced,‡
Two novel agencies are introduced:
By "Natural Selection" they profess
"Survival of the fittest" to express.
In life's rough race, the feeble lag behind,
The strong prevail, and propagate their kind.
Thus would the fittest, who alone survive,
At higher forms of life in time arrive.
This reas'ning failing, had to be revised,
And "Sexual Selection" was devised
To show that female animals possess
The sensual passions in refined excess:
Though males be wooers, females can reject,
And from the mass the favour'd one select.
Thus sexual lust all nature regulates,
And wanton matrons choose their ardent mates,

---

* 'Descent of Man,' vol. ii. pp. 238–384.
† Introduction, p. 11.   ‡ Ibid. p. 9.

The willing maidens favour handsome males,
So beauty triumphs, and love's power prevails.
This produce of selection and desire
Would forms more perfect gradually acquire.
This longing to be courted and admired,
Attained at last the end so much desired,—
By force of love, as Time his cycles ran,
A tiny tadpole grew to mighty Man.*

If this be true, no truth so true as this,
" That truth more strange than any fiction is."

These views, which scanned by an impartial eye
Seem monstrous from their great absurdity,—
As when the Elephant and Humming-bird †
Are to the same parental stock referred,—
To modern naturalists they appear
Simple and easy, quite correct and clear;
If evolution can the facts explain,
Then all is obvious, all distinct, and plain;
But if too subtle for the mind to grasp,
They baffle Reason, and evade its clasp,
Such to blind chance they instantly refer,—‡
At all allusion to " Design " demur.
Either they cannot or will not admit
That all things are ordained as seemeth fit
To an Almighty Power,—the great First Cause,
Who rules all Nature and all Nature's laws,
And caused all life such instincts to possess
As most conducive to its happiness,
And all its actions so to regulate
As to retain its pristine perfect state.

---

* 'Descent of Man,' vol. i. p. 205.   † See Note II.—Page 46.
‡ See Introduction, p. 16.

The facts they so triumphantly produce
In favour of their views, we too adduce
As confirmation of the mighty plan
In constant action since the world began,
By which the course of nature is arranged
To ever rest unaltered and unchanged.
Survival of the fittest, sexual choice,
In which the Evolutionists rejoice,
Are but the agents with which Nature works,
And in whose acts the deepest mystery lurks ;
Not to transform a fish into a bird,
And outrage nature with a hideous herd
Of half-formed monsters of untimely birth,
Encumb'ring and disfiguring the earth ;
But to sustain the vigour of all life
Against the inroads of disease and strife,
And so to bring the instincts into play
As to protect all nature from decay :
Each race from *retrogression* to preserve,
But not beyond its pristine state to swerve.
It is on means so suited to their ends,
The preservation of all life depends.

Yet such the doctrine now so boldly taught,
*Which sets the Bible and its Word at naught,
Treats it as fiction, for the simple mind
A pleasant fable ; but far, far behind
Our present knowledge, and with no pretence
To learning in a scientific sense.
'Twas but a poet's fancy to imply
That Man could be enlightened from on high,
Or that on Newton's mind a single ray
Or spark of Heav'nly fire could find its way.

---

* See Introduction, p. 17.

C

Such is the creed, where science reigns supreme,
And God is but the "fabric of a dream :"*
Where men, relying on their strength alone,
Judge the Almighty's Power by their own,
And, with the Laws of Nature not content,
New systems of their own device invent :
Reason unaided, thus obscures the light,—
All is confusion, all again is Night.

---

* See Note III.—Page 47.

PART II.

Not so with those who Faith with Reason blend,
Own a Beginning, and can see no End;
Learning respect, and scientific lore,
Revere the Sage, but love their Maker more:
Accept all truths deep study has explored,
And facts disclosed, in Nature's workshops stored.
But when vain man endeavours in his pride
Th' inspired Word of God to set aside,
Not for one moment question which is right,—
The wisdom finite, or the Infinite.

Why should we strive or wish to have it solved
How an Ascídi into Man evolved? *
Could not the Power who bade the Theyton live,
To man at once his perfect structure give?
It needs no complex system to explain
A fact at once so obvious and so plain.
In all things living, deep research can trace
A normal germ of life,—a common base
Of structural form in ev'ry class and race,—
On which, as on sweet music's gov'rning key,
All were created in strict harmony;
Some from the others diff'ring in degree
So slight as tests our utmost powers to see.
And though brute instinct and the human mind
Are wholly sep'rate and distinct, can find
That beasts a minor form of sense possess,
A feeble glimmer of self-consciousness,

* See Note IV.—Page 47.

In a material, not a moral sense,
As dread of punishment for an offence.
And certain other features can descry
Which both to man and animals apply.

But such resemblances we now are told
No scientific reason can uphold
Save by expansion from a common source,
Whilst countless ages rolled their ceaseless course.
Vain man! it is enough for you to know
It was God's pleasure to ordain it so;
His power is boundless, and is not confined
To the small compass of a finite mind.
For He who the Ascidian could create,*
Could also give to all things animate
Their attributes and forms as they now are,
Perfect at once in each particular.
And all research has failed as yet to show
A single case in which this was not so:
" Whilst of *transition* structure, not a clue †
Has e'er been found, or instance brought to view :"
The one is daily brought before our eyes,
The other 's all conjecture and surmise.
Why speculate what *may* or *might* have been,‡
When that which *is*, can be so plainly seen?

Such facts as these, if rightly learnt, disclose,
Not that one creature from another rose
Higher and higher, on a fancy plan
Designed by th' ingenuity of man;
But that in prodigality of power
God clothed the earth, and poured this living shower

---

* See Introduction, p. 19.   † See Note V.—Page 49.
† See Note VI.—Page 53.

Of varied form and beauty, to prepare
Our home beforehand with a loving care,
Replete with all that can delight the eye,
Our ev'ry want and ev'ry wish supply.

In these new systems we perceive no sign *
Of comprehensive purpose or design,
Though nature daily teaches us to see
For such design the great necessity :
If the exact proportions in all life †
Be not preserved to regulate the strife
Between all classes, then the slightest change
Would the nice balance wholly disarrange.
Mere sexual choice no order could maintain,
Nor such an equilibrium sustain :
Left to themselves, without a guiding hand
To regulate, restrain, direct, command,
All would collapse, the worst confusion reign,
And all to chaos would revert again.

Say, in all life, one general law pervades
The various classes and the various grades,
Yet all created perfect in their kind,‡
Each by itself, and to itself confined,
Each set his task, and his allotted beat,
One vast design, in all its parts complete ;
Then Faith joins Reason in her search for Light,
Leads her to Truth, and guides her steps aright:
The more she learns, the more she seeks to know,
At each advance, fresh proofs of goodness show,—
If in His wisdom God has much concealed,
Then faith supplies what He has not revealed.

-----

* See Note VII.—Page 54.   † See Note VIII.—Page 55.
‡ See Note IX.—Page 57.

But that Great Day, to which there is no night,
Shall solve all doubts in everlasting light:
All that is now obscure will then be clear
In the bright radiance of the Heav'nly sphere;
Whilst countless proofs of Wisdom, Power, and Love,
Meet our enraptured gaze where'er we move.
Then shall we know how vain it was for man
To strive, unaided, God's designs to scan;
His Might to question, and His Wisdom doubt,
" Whose ways are hidden, and past finding out;"
How vain to test Creation's mighty plan
By the same laws which rule the works of man;
Or gauge Almighty Power with Man's small rod,—
For are not all things possible with God,
Whose way is on the sea, whose paths alone
Cross the great deep, whose footsteps are not known?
Then shall we join the great adoring throngs,
Who raise their voices in unceasing songs
Of praise to Him, by whom the heavens were made,
And of the earth the deep foundations laid—
The Mighty God, who gave creation birth,
And breathed the breath of life o'er Heaven and Earth :
He spake,—earth, air, and sea the mandate heard,
And teemed with life responsive to His Word.
All things He made; but, ere his rest began,
In His own image He created man. *

---

* See Note X.—Page 58.

PART III.

They who the monad theory maintain,
At any ref'rence to God's Word complain.
It is no question of belief, they say,—
Solely of science; but, if so, can they
The Word of God contemptuously pass by,
And not the God who spake the Word deny?
Dare we select what portions to believe,
What to reject, and what as Truth receive,
May each of us admit what suits his views,
And credence to another part refuse,
Because its statements it does not profess
In scientific language to express?
Remove each part each doubter would erase,
Correct each sentence, and revise each phrase,
Disarm all cavil with the tend'rest care
By alterations here, omissions there;
Of all disputed portions thus bereft,
What of the sacred volume would be left?
Are the great truths and doctrines it affirms,
Of dubious meaning or in doubtful terms?
Are the great facts with which that Book is fraught
Mere idle tales, not worth a serious thought?

So when it tells us, " God created man
In his own image," no assertion can
Be more explicit; yet the modern sage
Would trace his lineage from the lowest stage
Of living forms. The two can *not* agree:
If one is right, wrong must the other be.*
The one asserts distinctly as a fact
That man's creation was a sep'rate act;

---

* See Note XI.—Page 60.

The other, that through all the grades he passed,
Of fishes, reptiles, birds, to man at last.
And one construction only can be placed
On words so plain, on facts so boldly traced.
As one and one make two, man can't, we know,
To both these sources his creation owe.
No sophism can these statements reconcile,
As diff'rence of expression, or of style:
To lay on lit'ral meaning so much stress
Is not borne out by fact, is profitless.
'Tis but a poor endeavour to evade
The charge of scepticism being made.
Better at once throw off the mask, than thus
Profess belief, and quietly discuss
Man's origin, as if not God, but Man
Had settled and arranged Creation's plan ;
As if to man's research alone, we owe
All of the world's creation that we know ;
As if the laws of nature disagreed
With what in God's inspired Word we read.

For not alone man's frame they now assume
To be from brutes developed, but presume
To rate the reason of the human mind,
As diff'ring in degree but not in kind,
From that of mammals of the higher class ;
And thence by graduations slow to pass
Lower and lower, through the meaner forms,—
Amphibians, fishes, molluscs, down to worms.
Sensation, instinct, reason, moral sense,
Knowledge of right and wrong, guilt, innocence,
One series form ; one from the other grew,
To " Natural Selection " all are due.*

---

* See Note XII.—Page 60.

If an immortal soul for man we claim,
We must for animals admit the same;
For fundamental diff'rence, not the least *
Exists between the minds of man and beast.
All may man's mighty intellect acquire,
And all to his high moral sense aspire.†
Man's mind and body thus alike are made
To rise together from the lowest grade.

These maxims lead to others of like kind,
Which show the progress of the human mind,—
Conscience, the prize of social happiness;
Remorse, regret at failure of success;
Right means the general good, or else what seemed ‡
To be so at the time; and wrong is deemed
A selfish instinct, which another's harm
Might consummate, and all regret disarm,
If instinct or desire the action bade,§
Which, to the mind, the social ties outweighed.
Right may be wrong; wrong right be deemed to be;
Killing no murder, theft no robbery.
Man placed in the position of the bee,‖
Without remorse would kill his progeny;
Mothers would daughters; sisters, brothers kill
And think a sacred duty they fulfil.
The "Social Instincts" the sole rule of life
To guide us through this world of sin and strife.
The poet's fancy strayed beyond recall,
Who sang of man's temptation, and his fall:
His wondrous epic was composed in vain,—
There was no Paradise, to lose or gain.

---

* See Note XIII.—Page 60. § See Note XVI.—Page 61.
† See Note XIV.—Page 61. ‖ See Note XVII.—Page 62.
‡ See Note XV.—Page 61.

Such are the axioms of the modern creed,*
From ev'ry trammel of religion freed;
Such are the lessons which their precepts teach,
Such the example to our youths they preach;
Such is the moral code by man designed,
To meet the wants and duties of mankind.
It needs no great discernment to foresee
What, with such rules of life, the end must be.
In such a creed the Sabbath's but a name,
Which has to any law divine no claim;
It can with science no connexion trace,
In "Natural Selection" finds no place
The "Evolution Doctrine," can suggest
No reason for a day of holy rest.
T' oppose such doctrines, each should do his best,†
And not resign his faith at the behest
Of man's conjecture; but at once refuse
All compromise, and every effort use
To frustrate the attempts now made to throw
Discredit on the Book to which we owe
All we hold dear, and on which rely
For all our hopes of Immortality.

This is no time the Gospel truths to hide,
With Infidelity on ev'ry side,—‡
A mighty host, with Science for its chief,
Sapping the very root of our belief.
Religion in our school-rooms set at naught,
The Bible scarce permitted to be taught;
True knowledge of its word placed out of reach,
Whilst sects are fighting for the right to teach.§
Our rising youth in ev'ry science skilled,
All duties to their God left unfulfilled:

---

* See Note XVIII.—Page 63.   ‡ See Note XX.—Page 66.
† See Note XIX.—Page 65.   § See Note XXI.—Page 67.

Wise in all ways, except the way of life;
Dead to all good, for ev'ry mischief rife.
With Faith a myth, morality a snare,
Virtue a sham, and scoffers everywhere.
Such must be, where *utility* is taught *
As the great object of a Nation's thought;
Such must be, where *the* Book, our only guide,
Is at the call of Science set aside;
Such the result with countries who have trod
The path of REASON, heedless of a God; †
But, praised be God, though black may be the cloud
That wraps our Nation in its sable shroud;
Though doubly dark and dreary be the Night
That spreads her sombre curtain o'er the Light;
Though scoffers go with sceptics hand in hand,
And Infidelity pervade the land;
Yet short and fruitless shall their triumph be
Who think the downfall of our faith to see.
The cloud will lift, the night will pass away,
A brighter light will usher in the day
When, purified and chastened in the fire
Of trouble, and affliction, and the ire
Of an offended God, we turn again
To Him, who can alone assuage our pain:
Before whose face, grim Unbelief shall quail,
All doubts shall vanish, and Great Truth prevail.

---

* See Note XXII.—Page 68.   † See Note XXIII.—Page 68.

NOTES.

NOTE I.—Page 30.

" Their gorgeous plumage artfully displayed."

MR. DARWIN devotes 200 pages of the Second Volume of the 'Descent of Man' to an elaborate description of the loves of birds, and 75 pages to that of beasts, and in relating the manner in which the more brilliantly and beautifully plumaged birds, such as the Peacock, the Argus Pheasant, the Turkey Cock, &c., display their plumage before the females, each in the precise manner best calculated to show off their beauty to the greatest advantage— the mammals also parading themselves in their courtships. Speaking of the Argus Pheasant, Mr. Darwin says :—" The Argus Pheasant does not possess brilliant colours, so that his success in courtship appears to have depended on the great size of his plumes, and on the elaboration of the most elegant patterns. Many will declare that it is utterly incredible that a female bird should be able to appreciate fine shades and exquisite patterns. Nevertheless, it is a marvellous fact that she should possess this almost human degree of taste, though perhaps she admires the general effect rather than each separate detail" (vol. ii. p. 93). In the Introduction we have shown that Mr. Darwin considers an apparent incompleteness in the upper ocellus in one of the secondary row of feathers of this bird as a proof that it could not have been the act of a separate creation, but that it must be in the course of being finished during some successive generations.

The strange antics performed by birds in their courtships are also given in great detail. " The great English bustard throws himself into indescribably odd attitudes whilst courting the female. An allied Indian bustard rises perpendicularly into the air with a hurried flapping of his wings, raising his crest, and puffing out the feathers of his neck and breast, and then drops to the ground. Such females as happen to be near obey the saltatory summons." Herons are described as walking about on their long legs with great dignity, bidding defiance to their rivals. And even of the disgusting carrion vulture it is said " that the gesticulations and parades of the males at the beginning of the love season are extremely ludicrous." Humorous descriptions are given of the love " Partridge dances " in North America, and of the " Rupicola crocea " at one of their meeting-places, at which ten males and two females were present, and where, as observed by Sir R. Schomburgk, a male "was capering to the apparent delight of several others."

The above extracts will serve to show the stress that is laid on these love displays of birds. And those of animals are equally dilated on, but for which we have no space, but must refer to the ' Descent of Man,' vol. ii. pages 38 to 315.

On this portion of Mr. Darwin's book, the writer in the ' Edinburgh Review ' for July, 1871, makes the following remarks :—" But we do Mr. Darwin no injustice in ascribing to him the theory of Lucretius, that Venus is the creative power of the world, and that the mysterious law of reproduction, with the passions which belong to it, is the dominant force of life. *He appears to see nothing beyond it, or above it.* In a Heathen Poet such doctrines appear gross and degrading, if not vicious; we know not how to characterize them in an English naturalist, well known for the purity and elevation of his life and character."

The above remarks do not so much refer to the descriptions given by Mr. Darwin, for they are chiefly taken from the accounts given by other travellers and naturalists, but to the conclusions drawn from them, which seem to amount to this,—that the beautiful plumage of birds, if not their powers of song, have been gradually acquired through the medium of Sexual Selection, from the males striving to appear as attractive as possible in the eyes of the females,

except in one small class, in which it is the females who
so strive, not the males. But as, in the course of ages,
sameness produced satiety, some bird, more daring than
the rest, by some wonderful effort of will, half-transformed
himself into an animal; and this bird-beast having thus
become more than ever attractive to the females, the
transformation went gradually on until the form of a per-
fect beast was acquired, and so on, and so on, to—MAN.
This is, indeed, a practical demonstration that "Venus is
the creative power of the World."

Mr. Darwin thus concludes his summary of his four
chapters on the sexual selection of birds:—"Finally, from
the facts given in these four chapters, we may conclude
that weapons for battle" (for there are regular laws of battle
for birds and mammals), "organs for producing sound, orna-
ments of many kinds, bright and conspicuous colours, have
generally been acquired by the males through 'Sexual
Selection,' and have been transmitted in various ways
according to the several laws of inheritance."—*Descent
of Man*, vol. ii. p. 238.

These views are intended to supersede our belief that
God created all things both for beauty and use, and gave
them all their separate instincts, by the exercise of which
all life is enabled to sustain itself in the perfect state in
which it was originally created. We leave the reader to
judge which conclusion accords best with common sense
and with known facts.

NOTE II.—Page 32.

"As when the Elephant and Humming-bird."

" The belief that animals so distinct as a monkey, or an
elephant, and a humming-bird, a snake, frog, and fish, &c.,
could all have sprung from the same parents, will appear
monstrous to those who have not attended to the recent
progress of natural history. For this belief implies the
former existence of links closely binding together all these
forms, now so utterly distinct. Nevertheless, it is certain
that groups of animals have existed, or do now exist, which

serve to connect more or less closely the several great vertebrate classes."—*Descent of Man*, vol. i. p. 203.

NOTE III.—Page 34.

"And God is but the 'fabric of a dream.'"

In a review of the 'Descent of Man' in the 'Edinburgh Review' for July, 1871, a long quotation is given from vol. i. p. 68 on the Mental Faculties of Man, on which the reviewer remarks : "So far as we can gather the meaning of this remarkable passage, our idea of God is a mere reflexion of ourselves without objective reality, the inevitable result of the activity of our minds." And in another passage the reviewer says : "Mr. Darwin states that his argument does not touch the existence of a God; but it completely destroys the objective value of any idea which we can form of Him, and this practically amounts to the same thing."

If these are, indeed, the modern naturalist's idea of God, the words of the text are fully borne out.

NOTE IV.—Page 35.

"How an Ascídi into Man evolved."

Cuvier, in his 'Règne Animal,' describes the Ascidians as molluscs of the order of "Naked Acephala." Mr. Darwin states (vol. i. p. 205) that "they belong to the Molluscoida of Huxley—a lower division of the great kingdom of the Mollusca ; but they have recently been placed by some naturalists amongst the Vermes, or worms ;" and thus describes them :—"invertebrate, hermaphrodite, marine creatures, permanently attached to a support. They hardly appear like animals, and consist of a simple, tough, leathery sack, with two small projecting orifices," "their larvæ somewhat resemble tadpoles in shape, and have the power of swimming freely about."

The Ascidians are very remarkable creatures in many respects. Remarkable, indeed, as we are told to look upon them as our remote progenitors ! It was a "happy thought" to fix upon an hermaphrodite animal as our original parent, a kind of joint-stock, grandfather and grandmother in one, as it saved the trouble of creating two beings, even for the two sexes,—the climax of the non-separate creation theory. There is another very remarkable feature in their case. We have always understood that "like breeds like," that the offspring, when arrived at maturity, must resemble the parent, or, as Cuvier remarks, "the species would become extinct." But some foreign naturalists have discovered that the larvæ of these *invertebrate* animals "are *related* to the *vertebrata* in the manner of their development, in the relative position of the nervous system, and in possessing a structure closely like the *chorda dorsalis* of vertebrate animals." Here, then, we have the larva of an animal differing in the *most important* point from its parent; and, as the vertebrata are a far higher class of animals than the invertebrata, we have the offspring *retrograding* in the scale of animal life as it arrives at maturity—as the statement is made of the larvæ of Ascidians in general, not of *one* particular specimen. So we have the curious fact of a creature producing something of a class vastly superior to itself; but that this superiority is confined to the period of its youth,—in mature years it is to degenerate into its parent's low estate.

Again, Mr. Darwin saw these larvæ, which resemble tadpoles in shape, swimming freely about. Happy spring-time of youth! for, after a time, they either become voluntary captives, or are compelled to be fettered for life, by becoming firmly attached to a support.

But Mr. Darwin says that "this larva, with its *chorda dorsalis*, has at last given us a clue to the source whence the Vertebrata have been derived" (vol. i. p. 205). So we must suppose that some one of these young Ascidians, not relishing the idea of being made a prisoner for life, being fond of peregrination, and having an enquiring mind, refused to be tied up; but starting forth on his travels, converted by mere strength of will his *chorda dorsalis*, which was at first only *closely like* that of vertebrate animals, into a real vertebral column, split himself into two, so that each half should possess one sex, and thus having acquired the powers of Sexual Selection, as well as of Natural Selection, was never satisfied until he stood up on his hind legs, got a smooth skin, and called himself Man.

If all this be so, it may well be said that " Truth is stranger than fiction ! "

NOTE V.—Page 36.

" Whilst of *transition* structure, not a clue."

That no fossil remains have ever been found of any animals in a state of transition from one class of animal life to another, has justly been considered as a strong argument against such gradual or insensible transformations having occurred. To which it is replied, that so small a portion of the earth's surface has been examined, that it may well be believed that such remains do exist, although they have not yet been brought to light.

But it is clear that this argument would apply to any monstrosity, however absurd, that anyone might say he had good reason for believing had at one time existed, and cannot be taken as worth much. The instances noticed by Mr. Darwin do not, in our opinion, help his case. He says, " We have seen that the Ornithorhynchus graduates towards reptiles ; and Professor Huxley has made the remarkable discovery that the old Dinosaurians are intermediate in many important respects between certain reptiles and certain birds—the latter consisting of the ostrich-tribe, and of the Archeopteryx, that strange Secondary bird having a long tail like that of the lizard. Again, the Ichthyosaurus, or fish-lizard, presents many affinities with fishes " (hence its name).—*Descent of Man*, vol. i. p. 204.

These remains simply show that such animals once existed, and formed part of that wonderful variety of animal and reptile life that we now see around us. But there is no proof to show that these animals were ever

D

anything but what their remains show them to have been, or that they were in a state of transition from one class of animal life to another class.

But, on the other hand, the fossil remains of extinct animals, which have been found in various parts of the world, appear to us to offer strong arguments against the Darwinian theory. The theory of Natural and Sexual Selection is, that the *fittest*, the strongest, the most perfect, the handsomest, the best of animal life, are those which come victorious out of the great battle of life, and by which the species and races are propagated, and so insensibly improved, as in course of years to pass from one species and class into other species and classes of a higher order by what is called evolution.

Let us consider some of these extinct animals, and see in how far they accord with this theory.

There is the fossil elephant, found entire, on the borders of the Icy Sea, near the mouth of the Lena, whose tusks were nine feet in length, and whose skull, without the tusks, weighed four hundred pounds.

Then there is the Great Mastodon,—that mighty monster, declared by Buffon to have been larger than any known terrestrial animal, whose habitat was supposed to have been the centre of the frozen zone.

Is the elephant, the only living representative of these great animals, superior to them in every respect? If not, how is it, by the law of the " *survival of the fittest*," these animals have become extinct, and the elephant remains, when there are still the frozen zone, and the borders of the Icy Sea, offering habitation for them?

Then there is the " Megatherium,"—that armour-clad monster, twelve feet long, and eight feet high, with feet a yard in length, partaking of the characters of the Sloth and of the Armadillo—of which Dr. Buckland says, " Secure within the panoply of his horny armour, where was the enemy who would dare encounter this Behemoth of the Pampas? or in what more powerful animal can we find the cause that has effected the extirpation of his race?"—*Bridgewater Treatises*, 'Geology,' vol. i. p. 164. This animal lived on roots—roots still exist—was he not the "fittest" of his race, or did the females prove unkind to him? What shall we say of the gigantic Dinotherium, the largest of terrestrial mammalia, supposed, from its remains, to have been eighteen feet in length, of the Tapir family? Are there now no freshwater lakes or rivers in which he could disport himself? By the laws of natural and sexual selection, how did this giant of mammals become extinct? There is the Megalosaurus, an enormous reptile, fifty feet in length, partaking of the structure of the crocodile and of the monitor—why is *he* extinct, and the crocodile living?

The Iguanodon, a monstrous herbivorous reptile, *seventy feet* in length—how has he retrograded into the present iguano, of from three to five feet long?

What shall we say of the Ichthyosaurus, the voracious fish-lizard, thirty feet in length, the orbital cavity of the eye measuring fourteen inches in its largest diameter, the size of a dinner-plate, with jaws six feet in length, full of fearful teeth, sometimes one hundred and eighty in number? With its extraordinary powers of locomotion, its wonderful arrangements for long or short sight, its large powerful jaws and teeth, what porpoise or grampus could compete with it? on what laws of the survival of the "fittest" has it become extinct, and the porpoise in its place? Is this progression or retrogression?

The "Plesiosaurus" is another remarkable example— "It had the head of a lizard, the teeth of a crocodile, a neck of enormous length, containing thirty-three vertebræ (a Camelopard has only seven); resembling the body of a serpent, a trunk and tail like an ordinary quadruped, the ribs of a chameleon, and the paddles of a whale."— *Buckland*, vol. i. p. 202.

On the principles of "Natural and Sexual Selection," how did this compound animal obtain its form? what was it evolved from? a fish! reptile! beast! or from all three at once?

Among birds, we may mention the footsteps of a bird twice the size of an ostrich. The fossil remains of many other extraordinary animals might be noticed, but we have only space for one, the "Pterodactyle," or flying lizard, which Cuvier considered by far the most wonderful animal that any fossil remains have brought to light,—a kind of bat or vampire, with an elongated snout like a crocodile, with the power of swimming and climbing, or creeping, or of suspending itself from trees, showing, as Dr. Buckland observes—as is the case with the other wonderful animals above noticed,—"a concurrence of proportions which it seems impossible to refer to the effect of accident, and which point out unity of purpose and deliberate design in some intelligent First Cause, from which they were all derived."

We have dwelt at considerable length on this subject, because we cannot see how these extraordinary animals, whose precise structures have, through the aid of man's research, been placed before our eyes, and some of which combined in one animal the structure of four or five totally different animals, could by any possibility have been produced from a common parent. Natural selection and sexual selection are completely at fault in the case of these compound creatures; and, as we are told by Mr. Darwin "that if any single link in this chain had not existed, man would not have been exactly what he is" (vol. i. p. 213), what part of the chain do these compound animals occupy in the "Descent of Man"?

And, as so much stress is laid upon the small extent of the earth's surface over which fossils have as yet been found, how do we know that the remains of many more creatures, each bearing in its frame the peculiar structure of several different animals that could not have been evolved from any single individual, may not yet be found?

Whilst, then, these remains appear to be perfectly incompatible with a gradual and insensible change of one creature into another of a different kind, they are consistent with all we know of the laws of creation, and of the omnipotent and beneficent Being, who, as we believe, laid the foundations of the earth, and from the beginning commenced preparing it with unerring wisdom and design for the occupation of man; and that all the changes in the constitution of the earth's crust, all the varieties of animal life, which naturalists and men of science have discovered, are all parts of one great system of perfect unity and design.

NOTE VI.—Page 36.

"Why speculate what *may* or *might* have been?"

In the review of the 'Descent of Man,' in the 'Times' of the 8th of April, 1871, the writer says, "The proper scientific mood is the Indicative; Science tells us 'what has been,' 'what is,' and 'what will be.' But Mr. Darwin's argument is a continuous conjugation of the Potential Mood. It rings the changes on 'can have been,' 'might have been,' 'would have been, should have been,' until it leaps with a bound into 'must have been.' We are at a loss to understand all this guesswork."

But as it is a law in all reasoning, that, "when known causes are sufficient to account for any phenomena, we shall not gratuitously call in additional cases" (*Quarterly Review*, July, 1871), we cannot see the object of all this speculation, when we know what really was, and is. These conjectures are unaccompanied by any direct evidence; for, as before remarked in our Introduction, the resemblances in the structures and habits of different animals and of man, are no proof whatever of their not having been separately created—of which the instances recorded in the last Note are a strong corroboration; whilst the account given of the creation of animal life in the Bible is perfectly consistent with everything in nature as it now exists—in so far as it pleased the Almighty to reveal it to us.

The heavens are very slightly alluded to. "He made the greater light to rule the day." "And the lesser light to rule the night." "He made the stars also." Yet,

although man has been permitted to search into the vast
heavenly expanse, and acquire for himself a thorough
knowledge of the size, the position, the motion, almost
the structure, of the innumerable worlds that revolve
through infinite space, nothing that the most powerful
instruments, or the highest efforts of mind, have enabled
him to discover, militates in the slightest degree against
the little it was thought necessary to inform man of in
the Bible narrative.   But the history of the creation of all
animal life, and of man, is given with great distinctness
and minuteness of detail; and whatever man, by his re-
searches into Nature's laws, past or present, may discover
in relation to animal life, although it must increase our
wonder at, and admiration of, "the power, wisdom, and
goodness of God," as displayed in all His works, can never
bring to light anything contrary to His revealed Word.

NOTE VII.—Page 37.

"In these new systems we perceive no sign."

Mr. Darwin, in his 'Origin of Species,' not only en-
dorsed Lamarck's theory of the evolution of one animal
into another of a different form, but attempted to show
that this development of animal life was brought about
by "natural selection," or the survival of the fittest.   In
his recent work, however, the 'Descent of Man,' he admits
that he greatly over-estimated the effects of natural selec-
tion, and so advances another new theory—that of "Sexual
Selection," which he asserts to be the real key to animal
life as it now exists, inclusive of man.   But he not only
derives man's physical structure from the lowest forms of
living beings, but does not hesitate to declare that man's
mental and intellectual faculties have also been gradually
developed from the sensations of the lower animals, from
which, he says, they differ "only in degree, not in kind."

Other naturalists and men of science, whilst they are
willing to admit that man, in his physical structure, *may*
have been developed from the lower animals, repudiate
the idea that man's intellectual faculties, and moral sense,

or conscience (which is the symbol of an immortal soul), have any relation whatever to the instincts of brutes.

If we accept the Darwinian theory, we must either believe that man, " the wonder of the universe," proceeded originally from the lowest type of animals, and that not only his animal nature, but his mental faculties, his moral sense, &c., are to be traced back to this lowest form of animal life; or we must believe that, whilst man in his animal nature was descended from these lowest forms of life, his mental powers and immortal soul were bestowed upon him direct from God.

In neither of these systems is there any comprehensive purpose or design; but simply that in some mysterious manner, a certain monad, or primitive form, was endowed with life, and the power given to it to develop itself during countless ages, from one stage of animal existence into another, until it became—Man. And this, not by any general law, but by individual efforts of natural and sexual selection,—the progress of the mind following that of the progress of the body. Or, if this last assumption is denied, we must believe that the animal called man,—though Mr. Darwin tells us " that we have nothing to guide us as to when that term should be applied,"—having, by the help of natural and sexual selection, arrived at his present form, God selected this animal, this product of the lucky chances of life, and of the waywardness of the lowest passions, this offspring of a " hairy animal with pointed ears, and a tail," as a fit temple in which to implant an immortal soul. And we are called upon to believe this, not on physical evidence, for there is none,—not a single instance or specimen of any animal in its progress of development being forthcoming—but on mere conjecture as to what may or might have been.

Note VIII.—Page 37.

" If the exact proportions in all life."

If it has been shown that there is no comprehensive purpose or design in the Darwinian theory, it is most clear to all observers of nature, that they both exist in the most marked manner in all the workings of Nature's laws that we see around us. All life may be nearly divided into two classes, one of which is the food of the other—so that there is a constant struggle for existence and subsistence going on; and this battle of life is waged by the most minute, as well as by the largest and most powerful of animal life. We see it in the water from a ditch, when exposed to a microscope of intense power,—we see a constant destruction and sustenance of the most minute forms of life, incessantly carried on: in the sea, on the earth, in the air, we perceive the same battle of life in progress; we see that certain classes of life depend entirely for their existence on certain other classes of life, and that if this, their food, should fail them, they would starve and become extinct. We see, also, that if the food multiplied beyond the powers of the feeders to consume it, it would, in its turn, so increase as to destroy all the vegetation on the earth on which it exists.

So that, in the thousands of classes of which animal life is composed, it is absolutely necessary that an exact balance should be preserved; otherwise the whole organism of nature would be destroyed.

All observers of nature must have noticed how that, owing to some, to us unknown causes, a certain class of animal life has for the time, and locally, so increased beyond its due proportion, as to threaten to overturn the course of nature; but how equally, without apparent cause, the classes which feed upon this former class, have suddenly made their appearance, no one knew from whence, and once more restored the balance to an equipoise. Blight, swarms of insects, the sudden flights of locusts, and the rapid increase of some of the smaller races of animals well known to naturalists, all confirm these views; and the mysterious manner in which these sudden disturbances are quelled is utterly beyond the control of individual action, and can only be accounted for by the ordinance of an omnipotent and beneficent Being, who thus regulates all nature, so as to secure the greatest good to all His creatures.

NOTE IX.—Page 37.

" Yet all created perfect in their kind."

It is scarcely necessary to observe that this line is in direct contradiction to the Darwinian theory, which asserts that all animals have a common parentage, or were gradually developed from one original germ. It may to many be equally unnecessary to point out that it is in perfect consonance with the views of the greatest comparative anatomist, Cuvier, who says in the introduction to his ' Règne Animal,' " We are thus compelled to admit of certain forms which from the origin of things have perpetuated themselves without exceeding these limits ;" and again, " *Fixed* forms that are perpetuated by generation, distinguish their species, determine the complication of the secondary functions proper to each of them, and assign to them the parts they are to play on the great stage of the universe. *These forms are neither produced nor changed by their own agency* ; life supposes their existence. Its flame can only be kindled in a frame already prepared, and the most profound meditation and lynx-eyed and delicate observation can penetrate no farther than the mystery of the pre-existence of the germs."

It is impossible for any conclusions to be more directly opposed to each other than those of M. Cuvier and Mr. Darwin ; and it must be left for those in any way acquainted with the subject to decide whether the conjectures, the imaginary beings, the possibilities, the " may be," " might be," of Mr. Darwin, are for a moment to be set against the precise reasoning, the wonderful powers of observation, the unequalled knowledge of comparative anatomy that Cuvier possessed and displayed in so marked a degree. We admit that since Cuvier's time many new facts have been observed, and much light thrown on many sections of natural history ; but we do not admit that anything discovered since his time is calculated to shake the fundamental principles of nature on which Cuvier grounded his conclusions; and before we send the "Règne Animal" to the confectioner's or the trunk-maker's, we must have something better to replace it on our book-shelves than the 'Descent of Man.'

NOTE X.—Page 38.

"In His own image He created man."

The reviewer of the 'Descent of Man' in the 'Edinburgh Review' for July, 1871, although he goes so far as to declare that "the doctrine of evolution has not the least bearing either in destroying the foundation of religious belief, or as an overwhelming argument in favour of materialism, and need not alarm the most timid theologian," and who also says, "that the doctrine of evolution *may* be the only reasonable explanation of the difference and resemblance of plants and animals, and of their distribution in space and time, but nevertheless that it must be admitted that its truth is as yet very far from being proved." Admitting all this, the reviewer is staggered at the idea of *man* in his present form having been produced solely by such an agent, and states "that Mr. Wallace, the founder of the theory of Natural Selection, has expressly excepted man from the action of what he believes to be a law to the rest of the organic world." The reviewer continues, "How can we tell that man has not arisen from his lowly ancestry suddenly, from the incidence of causes beyond the ken of the naturalist?" "How can we tell that he did *not spring forth suddenly*, as the manifestation of humanity in the brute creation?" "It may be that primeval man was closely linked to the ape in body, as we ourselves are, but we *deny that there is any evidence of an insensible graduation.*"

To "spring forth suddenly," without any sensible gradua-tion, is surely tantamount to a separate act of creation, and entirely opposed to the Darwinian theory. And as this separate act of creation agrees with the Bible narrative, to which the other is as directly opposed, we fail to see that the doctrine of evolution as applied to man, even according to this writer's view of it, has nothing to do with religious belief.

We have shown in Note IV. the horns of the dilemma on which naturalists are placed, who, declaring man in his physical structure to be an animal, admit the doctrine of evolution as regards all other animals, but except man; for if he is *bonâ fide* an animal, he would (admitting the doctrine of evolution) have been subjected to the same laws of insensible formation as other animals; but, if he was separately created, how comes it that his frame should, as it is stated, in every respect exactly conform to that of animals gradually arrived at after an indefinite period of time, through the chances and vagaries of natural and sexual selection?

And if this difficulty exists in regard to man's physical structure, it becomes far greater and far more serious when applied to his mental faculties and to his moral sense; for either we must believe that the immortal soul is a mere development of the lowest germ of sensation that exists in the inferior forms of animal life,—a belief which scarcely anyone is bold enough to acknowledge,—or we must believe that when animal life had arrived at a certain stage (for Mr. Darwin says "it would be impossible to fix on any definite time when the term *man* ought to be used"), and a certain animal had obtained a certain peculiar form and structure, and when the intellectual faculties of this particular animal had reached a certain point (for here again Mr. Darwin tells us that we need be under no anxiety as to *when* this occurred), the Deity then *again* took part in the scheme of creation, selected this uncouth animal (for such the *immediate offspring* of an ape, or of a hairy animal with pointed ears and a tail, must have been on the theory of insensible graduation, almost defenceless, very far inferior to numbers of other animals, both in beauty of form, in strength, in powers of defence and of attack), as the one above all others to endow with an immortal soul, and to hold personal communion with; &c.,

and this latter alternative is as repugnant to our feelings as the former.

Note XI.—Page 39.

"If one is right, wrong must the other be."

We have endeavoured to show, in our Introduction, how perfectly incompatible the Mosaic narrative and the Darwinian theory are, and that no sophism can reconcile them, and what must be the effect of accepting Mr. Darwin's conclusions; so we will merely state here that we have good cause to be jealous of any attempt to undermine our faith in the Bible, by the subtle introduction of the thin end of the wedge of unbelief; and although no open expression of disbelief is made, although the question of how man came into the world is declared to have no reference to religion, the very fact of contemptuously putting on one side, as unworthy of consideration, the account given in the Bible of the creation of man, and asserting in the most dogmatic language that man was produced in a totally different manner, is in *deed*, if not in word, expressing utter disbelief in the Word of God.

Note XII.—Page 40.

"To 'Natural Selection' all are due."

Mr. Darwin says, in his 'Descent of Man,' "Nevertheless, the first foundation or origin of the moral sense lies in the social instincts, and these instincts no doubt were primarily gained, as in the case of the lower animals, through *Natural Selection* " (vol. ii. p. 394).

Note XIII.—Page 41.

"For fundamental difference, not the least."

" My object in this chapter is solely to show that there is no fundamental difference between man and the higher mammals in their mental faculties."—*Descent of Man*, vol. i. p. 35.

Note XIV.—Page 41.

" And all to his high moral sense aspire."

" The following proposition seems to me in a high degree probable, namely, that any animal whatever, endowed with well-marked social instincts, would *inevitably* acquire a moral sense or conscience as soon as its intellectual powers had become as well developed, or nearly as well developed, as in man."—*Descent of Man*, vol. i. p. 71. On which the Edinburgh Reviewer remarks, " Mr. Darwin's theory of the growth of the moral sense, and of the intellectual faculty, is unsupported by any proofs."

Note XV.—Page 41.

" Right means the general good, or else what seemed."

" And thus our sense of right and wrong is gradually evolved by *natural selection*, without the *necessity* of the *interference of any other laws*. It is merely the result of the working of the principle of utility in our nature. Right is merely what is found to be by experience for the good of society ; and wrong, that which is hurtful, or is deemed to be so."—*Edinburgh Review*, on ' Descent of Man.'

Note XVI.—Page 41.

" If instinct or desire the action bade."

" If any instinct or desire leading to an action opposed to the good of others still appears to a man, when recalled to mind, as strong as or stronger than his social instinct, he will find no keen regret at having followed it."—*Descent of Man*, vol. i. p. 92.

" It is obvious that any one may with an easy conscience gratify his own desires, if they do not interfere with his social instincts, that is, with the good of others." —*Ibid*. vol. i. p. 92.

Mr. Darwin attempts to somewhat qualify this proposition ; but the whole bent of his argument is to show that man's actions are to be considered right or wrong, not in any way as his acts affect his duty to God as an individual, but as they affect the general good of the society in which he lives.

Note XVII.—Page 41.

"Man placed in the position of the bee."

"If, for instance, to take an extreme case, men were reared under precisely the same conditions as hive bees, there *can hardly be a doubt* that our unmarried females would, like the worker-bees, think it a sacred duty to kill their brothers, and mothers would strive to kill their fertile daughters, and no one would think of interfering." —*Descent of Man*, vol. i. p. 73. On which the critic in the 'Times' of April 8th, 1871, very justly remarks, "What is this but to place every barrier of moral obligation at the mercy of the conditions of life? Men unfortunately have the power of acting not according to what is their ultimate social interest, but according to their ideas of it; and if the doctrine could be impressed on them that right and wrong have no other meaning than the pursuit or the neglect of their ultimate interest, conscience would cease to be a check upon the wildest, or, as Mr. Darwin's own illustration allows us to add, the most murderous revolutions. At a moment when every artificial principle of authority seems undermined, we have no other guarantee for the order and peace of life except in the eternal authority of those elementary principles of duty which are independent of all times and of all circumstances." And the reviewer in the 'Edinburgh Review' for July, 1871, thus comments on this passage of the bees :—"The sense of right and wrong, according to this view, is no definite quality, but merely the result of the working together of a series of accidents controlled by natural selection, for the general good. We need hardly point out that, if this doctrine were to become popular, the constitution of society would be destroyed; for if there be no objective right and wrong, why should we follow one instinct more than the others, excepting so far as it is of direct use to ourselves?"

Note XVIII.—Page 41.

"Such are the axioms of the modern creed."

It must be apparent to everyone who has given any attention to this subject, that the axioms here propounded are totally opposed to all our preconceived opinions. Reason and instinct are treated as being derived from the same primary sensations. "There is no fundamental difference between the mental faculties of man and animals;" "and it deserves notice that we here find the *intellectual faculties* developed, but in two very distinct lines, to the highest standard, namely, in the Hymenoptera (ants, bees, &c.), amongst the Anthropoda, and in the Mammalia, including man, amongst the Vertebrata."—*Descent of Man*, vol. ii. p. 396. Thus we are told that the *intellectual faculties* are developed to the highest standard in *ants* and *bees*, and it is attempted to be shown that instinct gradually developes into reason, and into moral sense or conscience.

But Cuvier, in his 'Règne Animal,' gives a very different definition of "instinct" and reason. Whilst admitting that the higher animals possess a certain degree of reason, which at the bottom of the scale is reduced to equivocal signs of sensibility, he describes "instinct" as another kind of intelligence, "often also very complicated, and which if *attributed to intelligence* would suppose a foresight and knowledge in the species that perform them infinitely superior to what can possibly be admitted. This instinct increases in proportion as the animals belong to the less elevated classes, and their actions are so entirely the property of the species that all its individuals perform them in the same way, *without ever improving them a particle*," and, to illustrate this, the *instincts* of bees and of wasps is particularly referred to.

Cuvier adds, that "the impression of external objects upon an individual, the production of a sensation or of an image, is a mystery into which the human understanding cannot penetrate, and *materialism is an hypothesis so con-jectural*, that philosophy can furnish no direct proof of the actual existence of matter."

Mr. Darwin and others of the modern school of philo-sophy assert that our high intellectual faculties have been gradually developed, and " the greater number of the more complex instincts appear to have been gained in a wholly different manner, through the natural selection of variations of simpler instinctive actions. We can, I think, come to no other conclusion with respect to the origin of the more complex instincts, when we reflect on the marvellous in-stincts of sterile worker-ants and bees, who leave no offspring to inherit the effect of experience and of modified habits." " In this latter case " (that of actions instinctively performed by the lower animals) "the capacity for performing such actions having been gained *step by step*," &c.—*Descent of Man*, vol. i. pp. 38, 39.

Is there any—even the slightest—proof that the sterile ants and bees *have improved in their instinct*, or anything but mere conjecture that they have so done, or that these. instincts were only acquired by ants and bees when by natural selection they had been evolved from some less perfect insect with less perfect instincts? Which is most compatible with reason, with common sense, and with all that we see around us,—Cuvier's statement that instinct acts *always* in the same way, and never *improves* a particle, or that it has been brought to perfection *step by step* by " natural selections "? We leave this new discovery of modern naturalists to the judgment of our readers.

But the connexion of the moral sense of man with the instinct of animals is a far more serious question. Attri-buting all our actions to the workings of social instincts, which are in themselves due to natural selection, strikes at once at the very foundation of our religious belief. We have, in Note XIII., shown some of the consequences that would arise from the adoption of the moral code laid down in these views, and shall enlarge upon them in a subsequent Note.

Note XIX.—Page 42.

"To oppose such doctrines, each should do his best."

The reviewer in the 'Edinburgh Review' for July, 1871, says, "The comparison of the feeling of religious devotion in man with the emotion of dogs and monkeys would be unworthy of notice, had it been made by any man less distinguished than Mr. Darwin." Doubtless if a mere smatterer in natural history had advanced such views as Mr. Darwin has done, using hard words against those who presume to differ from him, his speculations would have been considered "as unworthy of notice." But coming from a person of such high repute in the scientific world, such a keen and accurate observer of nature, and of such high personal character, as to entitle him to speak authoritatively on the subject, and whose dicta will be accepted by many almost without inquiry, the assertions of such a man are infinitely more dangerous than if they were "beneath notice;" being calculated not only to generate false scientific views, but, by his astounding conclusions in regard to man's moral sense and the immortality of the soul, if not at once unhesitatingly put down, to have a most pernicious effect upon our social interests.

The same reviewer says, "It is indeed impossible to overestimate the magnitude of the issue. If our humanity be merely the natural product of the modified faculties of brutes, most earnest-minded men will be compelled to give up the motives by which they have attempted to live noble and virtuous lives as founded on a mistake; our moral sense will turn out to be a mere developed instinct, identical in kind with that of ants or bees, and the revelation of God to us, and the hope of a future life, pleasurable day-dreams invented for the good of society. If these views be true, a revolution in thought is imminent, which will shake society to its very foundation, by destroying the sanctity of the conscience and the religious sense,—for sooner or later they must find expression in their lives."— *Edinburgh Review*, for July, 1871.

E

The reviewer of the 'Descent of Man' in the 'Quarterly Review' for July, 1871, says, "If Mr. Darwin's failure should lead to an increase of philosophic culture on the part of physicians we may therein find some consolation for the *injurious effects* which his work is likely to produce on too many of our half-educated classes." And the review of the 'Descent of Man' in the 'Times' of April 8, 1871, concludes in these words :—"A man incurs a grave responsibility who, with the authority of a well-earned reputation, advances at such a time the disintegrating speculations of this book. He ought to be capable of supporting them by the most conclusive evidence. Such cursory investigation, such hypothetical arguments as we have exposed, is more than unscientific, it is reckless."

These are strong and well-deserved reproofs, and nothing that we could say would add to them. But the misfortune is that reviews are read and put on one side, and although at the time the effect they produce may be great, other objects and other interests soon engross the attention; whilst a standard book such as the 'Descent of Man,' the work of one of the leading naturalists and philosophers of the age, remains to inculcate its pernicious doctrines into the minds of hundreds of future readers, without the antidote being at hand, and therefore every effort should be made to strip the conclusions of their fascinating envelopment, and expose their materialistic principles in their true colours.

NOTE XX.—Page 42.

"With Infidelity on every side."

The state of religious feeling among the undergraduates and the professors in many of the colleges of our two great Universities, and of the increased attention now given to the teachings of Modern German and French, as well as of Modern English Philosophy, is unhappily too well known to require any comment. But the extent to which these feelings have arrived among those who have already entered upon the Battle of Life, the following extract from

a sermon preached by the Rev. Dr. Vaughan in the Temple Church, on the 22nd January, 1871, will show :—
" Men presume to assert—thank God we know it to be a falsehood, yet like most falsehoods it is founded on fact—that there is not to be found a young lawyer who believes; that this whole profession, taken as the sample and specimen of English intelligence, has renounced its faith in Christianity. God forbid! But the very assertion shows the abounding of infidelity; men durst not hazard the saying it, were there not such a large element of truth."

Such a statement, made in the Temple Church, in the very heart of the legal profession, by so distinguished a theologian, is of too grave import not to give occasion to serious misgivings.

NOTE XXI.—Page 42.

"Whilst sects are fighting for the right to teach."

The Education Act of the session of 1870 is too recent, and too well impressed upon all who are interested in the subject, for them not to remember the difficulty with which the concession was obtained for having the Bible read at all in our National schools, and the restrictions, almost amounting to prohibition, which were placed upon any explanation of it. Although we have the authority of Scripture for believing that the mere reading of the Bible without explanation, is to many but of little value; for when the Apostle Philip asked the Ethiopian eunuch, " Understandest thou what thou readest?" the earnest student of the Bible replied, "How can I, except some man should *guide* me?"

And that the spirit of opposition to the necessary teaching of God's Word has not yet died out, we have proofs every day to remind us. In the 'Times' of Nov. 17, 1871, we read, "The Norwich Nonconformists had a meeting last night, Mr. J. H. Tillett in the chair, at which the Elementary Education Act was condemned as unjust in some of its leading provisions, and as calculated to promote religious animosities. It was also intimated that if the

Nonconformists did not receive attention from the Government on the expression of their views, the Nonconformist members might retreat from the House of Commons upon some critical occasions."

This is truly fighting for the "right to teach;" and whilst these fights are going on, hundreds, nay thousands, of poor children will be deprived of all religious instruction, whilst the battle is waging for the right of saving their souls.

Note XXII.—Page 42.

"Such must be where *utility* is taught."

Placing Secular Education as the first thing to be considered in a scheme of National Education, sacrificing everything to "Utility," the dissemination of such principles as are inculcated in the 'Descent of Man,' and in the schools of Foreign Modern Philosophy, must in time bear their fruits, unless successfully combated by all those who love their religion and the prosperity of their country.

Note XXIII.—Page 43.

"The path of Reason, heedless of a God."

"There is too much reason to fear that loose philosophy, stimulated by an irrational religion, has done not a little to weaken the force of those principles in France, and that this is, at all events, one potent element in the disorganization of French Society."—*Review of* 'Descent of Man,' 'Times,' April 8, 1871.

GENERAL CONCLUSIONS.

EVENTS march now so rapidly, that since the foregoing pages were written several things have occurred to corroborate the views advanced in the text and notes, and which we propose to embody with some further elucidations of the subject.

On the 3rd March, 1872, Mr. Dixon brought forward his motion in the House of Commons condemnatory of the Government Education Act of 1870, and proposing the abolition of all religious teaching in Government Elementary Schools—on which the 'Times' of March 6th remarks, "They (the League) have now advanced to this point, that in the interest of freedom of conscience, men shall be compelled to send their children to schools where the teaching of religion in any degree must be rigorously disallowed, the teachers in which are indeed to be placed under a ban, and forbidden to teach the most elementary religious knowledge, even out of school hours.'

The result of a nation thus, as a nation, ignoring its God, can scarcely be doubtful, or if a doubt could exist on the subject, the result of such a system in France affords practical evidence that cannot be mistaken. The Marquis of Salisbury in a speech at Liverpool on the 5th April, 1872, said, " The report of the French National Assembly upon the cause of the terrible Commune Insurrection shows most distinctly that the cause which led to the disorganization of French Society was the decadence of the religious spirit in that nation, and that the decline in that religious spirit was due to the fact that religious teaching had been banished from their system of education."—' Daily News,' April 6th, 1872.

The state to which secular education, and materialistic

philosophy have reduced intellectual France may be further judged of by the following telegrams, published in the 'Times' of March 9th and 12th, 1872. "In to-day's sitting of the National Assembly, the Assembly rejected the proposal of M. Brunet for the erection of a temple to Jesus Christ in the Trocadero, as an expression of belief in God, which M. Brunet declared to be necessary for national regeneration." That a member of the National Assembly should consider it necessary to propose to the Assembly the erection of a temple as an expression of belief in God, is surely a sign of the times. And again, on March 11th, "The Committee on primary instruction informed M. Jules Simon to-day that it rejected the text of this Bill. M. Jules Simon said he would defend in the Assembly the existence of a moral system independent of the Gospel."

Surely the above extracts ought to open our eyes to the inevitable results of national education from which all religious teaching is excluded ; and on what possible grounds it can be expected that the system of purely secular education which an influential party are now striving to force upon this country, should not lead to the same results here as in France, we are at a loss to understand. The bearing of this system of secular education upon our subject is obvious, for to admit the Darwinian theory in its fullest sense, we must deny the Divine authority of the Scriptures, and it is only with a purely secularly educated people, that such a theory could hope to find acceptance.

It is very easy for some of the supporters of the Darwinian theory to pooh-pooh, or even to make a joke of the religious view of the question, and to say it cannot make any difference to us now, whether we owe our origin to a monad, to an ape, or to a direct act of creation ; that we are what we are, is what most concerns us. No doubt it is necessary for them thus to make light of its unscriptural conclusions, for the British public are not yet quite prepared to ignore their Bible; and although it may be said that the 'Descent of Man' is a purely scientific book, addressed to the scientific reader, and not to the general public; the moral and social doctrines it expounds are of such a character, that if accepted at first only by the better educated, they would in time influence every grade, and affect our whole social system.

And it does concern us as Christians to maintain intact our faith in the Bible, on which our belief in Christianity is founded, and not to allow its most important facts and truths to be tampered with to meet the views of any school of philosophy. Some of the unscriptural conclusions in the 'Descent of Man' have already been given, but one or two more may be adduced. Man's moral sense or conscience, is said to owe its first origin to the social instincts of animals, and the effect of this moral sense on his actions is thus described. "It is obvious that every one may with an easy conscience gratify his own desires, if they do not interfere with his social instincts, that is, with the good of others." This we have quoted in Note XVI., but it may be as well to finish the sentence, which is as follows:—"But in order to be quite free from self-reproach, or at least of anxiety, it is almost necessary for him to avoid the disapprobation, whether reasonable or not, of his fellow-men." "He must likewise avoid the reprobation of the one God or gods, in whom, according to his knowledge or superstition he may believe; but in this case the additional fear of divine punishment often supervenes" (vol. i. p. 93). There is not one word here of our actions being influenced by gratitude, or by love for that God who so loves us, but solely by fear of offending our fellow-men, or the one God or gods in whom we may believe—the fear of Divine punishment often supervening.   There was at one time, whether it exists now we know not, a sect called "Devil Worshippers," who went upon the principle that God was full of loving-kindness, too good, too merciful, to condemn any of his creatures to eternal punishment; but that it was the Devil who did this, so, said they, "let us worship the Devil and propitiate him."   We cannot subscribe to a theory which inculcates such doctrines as these.

Its morality may be judged of by the following extract, in which Mr. Darwin fully adopts the new system of competitive qualification, though in a sense not we imagine contemplated by the military authorities. Discussing the subject of the increase of mankind, under the head of sexual selection, he says, "There should be open competition for all men, and the most able should not be prevented by laws or customs from succeeding best, and rearing the largest number of offspring" (vol. ii. p. 403).

The Darwinian theory adopts the principle that nothing is to be admitted but what can be ascertained— for instance, whilst advancing the necessity of the general acceptance of some definition of the term species Mr. Darwin says, "And the definition must not include an element that cannot possibly be ascertained, such as an act of creation" (vol. i. p. 228).   If we are not to admit or to believe anything that we cannot now understand, or that cannot be precisely ascertained, then, indeed, do we renounce faith, which is the evidence of things *not* seen.

In arguing that man and all other animals have been constructed on the same general model, Mr. Darwin says, "Consequently we ought frankly to admit their community of descent; to take any other view is to admit that our own structure, and that of all the animals around us, is a mere snare laid to entrap our judgment" (vol. i. p. 32). We believe that man and all other animals were constructed with a perfect unity of design, or on the same general model; but we totally demur to their community of descent—that is, that they have all proceeded from one common stock. Are we then to be told that we admit that God so created all living things " as a snare laid to entrap our judgment; " if the sentence does not mean this, what does it mean?

The remark by Mr. Darwin that because we do not know when a child before or after birth becomes an immortal being, we need be under no more anxiety to know *when* man became so,—has been slightly referred to in our Introduction; but it may be further remarked here that the question is, not so much *when*, as *how*, man became an immortal being. It is admitted that there was a time when man, or some one of his progenitors, was not an immortal being, the question is *how*, according to the Darwinian theory, did he become so. Man could not have obtained an immortal soul by natural and sexual selection, but to admit that he became an immortal being by the direct intervention of the " one God or gods in whom according to our knowledge or superstition we may believe," would be fatal to the Darwinian theory, which forbids all extraneous interference, even for the creation of a species, and the very essence of which theory is, that the physical and mental powers, and faculties of man, and of all other animals, existed in the same embryo in the lower forms of life, and have, by some innate power, gradually by their own exertions, and by the constant exercise of that power, attained fresh powers, and eventually developed into their present state.

As we believe that the Darwinian theory as expounded in the 'Descent of Man,' succumbs to the above crucial test, it might have been dismissed as an ingenious speculative discussion, but for its bearing upon revealed religion—under any other view, it would be a matter of no interest or importance to us, to be told that we are descended from an hermaphrodite parent, or when, or how, the separation of the sexes was effected—this is an erudite point in natural history, the elucidation of which we would gladly leave for the amusement of the Darwinites; but when opinions are expressed and conclusions arrived at under the authority of a great name in the scientific world, which are directly opposed to facts recorded in Sacred Scripture, and which play into the hands, we believe most unintentionally on the part of their author, of a school of materialistic philosophy which would have us submit to see leaf after leaf torn from the Bible before our eyes, and to become in time, like the supposed skinned eels, rather to like it than otherwise. We say it is then time for all who love and value their religion, to come forward and expose the fallacies of such a doctrine.

The ground-work of the Darwinian theory as regards man, rests on the assumption that there is no fundamental difference between man and the higher mammals in their mental faculties, for otherwise " we should never have been able to convince ourselves that our high faculties have been gradually developed " (vol. i. p. 35). If, then, it can be shown that a fundamental difference between the mental faculties of man and animals does exist, the whole theory would fall to the ground.

The great characteristic of the mind of man is reason, that of animals is instinct. Instinct has been so often defined, and shown to be so totally distinct from, and independent of reason, that the arguments need not have been repeated here, were it merely a discussion regarding a point of scientific nomenclature, but as so much in the present case depends upon the exact meaning of the term, we must enlarge upon it. Some assert that there is only one instinct; some that there are simple and complex instincts; but we believe that the instinct which occupies the place in animals that reason does in man, is totally distinct from those universal natural impulses by which alone life is preserved, such as the impulse which enables the young to take its first nourishment, the act of swallowing, of moving the limbs, and such like, which are common to all animal life, man inclusive. The instinct by which bees and wasps make their combs, birds build their nests, and ants their wonderful habitations, beavers their canals and dams, &c., the instinct by which migratory birds wend their course through the trackless air, and fishes through the pathless ocean when they return to the same rivers to spawn; by which animals find their way across large tracts of country they have never before traversed; are faculties of a totally different nature from the mere natural impulses that preserve life, and instead of being universal and the same in all, are restricted to certain orders, and vary in every class, and man has no claim to any one of these true instincts—it is not that he does not possess it in such perfection as the lower animals, but he has it not at all. What is generally called instinct in man is simply those general natural impulses necessary for the immediate preservation of life; but the true special instinct of animals is replaced in man's mind by reason—the difference is not in degree but in kind.

But before proceeding to show that the mind of man does not owe its origin to the instincts of animals, it may be as well to point out some strong grounds against the mental faculties of animals having been derived one from the other, and if not their mental faculties, then that their physical structure has not. Like breeds like—similarity cannot evolve into dissimilarity—if the instinct of any animal is really derived from that of some animal, &c., below it in the organic scale, it would be of the same kind but improved—as evolution implies progress; but in the cases of the bee and the wasp, if these insects were not separately created, but proceeded one from the other, why are the instincts by which they are compelled, without any volition of their own, to construct their cells, so totally different—one bee secreting wax which another bee moulds into a cell, in which the egg of another is deposited; whilst the wasp makes her cells or nests of paper, deposits her egg, and then does what no bee ever does, brings a grub or grubs, and places them in the hole for the worm from the egg to feed upon? Neither of these insects has any idea why it does all this, or what is to be the result, the wasp even dying before the young come forth; it is not a question which shows the highest constructive power; the geometrical cell of the bee, or the beautiful paper of the wasp, both are equally adapted for the required end; but how could such opposite instincts have been derived one from the other? and if not the instincts, then the insects were not.

The totally different manner in which the various species of birds build their nests, is another example. If we ascend to mammals, from what animals did the beaver derive his marvellous instinct, and to what animal has it been transferred? Instinct has nothing to do with experience: it cannot be taught; it is not an act of imitation—being perfect at first it never improves—the bee one hour old flies to the flowers, collects the honey and pollen, and commences the necessary manipulations; the instinct of the sterile worker bee cannot be strictly inherited from that particular branch of the community, it can only be a direct gift from the Almighty; and the great Sir Isaac Newton went so far as to assert, " That the whole actions of the brutes are the constant, direct, and immediate operations of the Deity Himself." Without entering into this question, we conceive that everything shows that the instincts of animals are not derived one from the other; but that each animal has been endowed with an instinct best suited to its wants and enjoyment of life.

To accept the doctrine that one animal has been evolved from some other, we must suppose that, as it in time became greatly different from its progenitor, the instinct which was applicable to the one class of animal life died off, and another and totally different instinct was given. If so, by whom? The class of animals called ruminants offer a striking example. This class has the peculiar instinct of chewing the cud; it is not a natural impulse common to all animal life, but peculiar to this class—whence was it derived? In what possible manner can natural or sexual selection have produced the four stomachs in ruminants, the nerves and muscles necessary for withdrawing the food from the stomach to the mouth, the lateral action of the jaws necessary for masticating it, and all the elaborate contrivances by which this peculiar action is carried out? The survival of the fittest cannot have caused it, for in what respect are the ruminants superior to the non-ruminants? in what respect is the ox superior to the horse? If it is said by having horns, the camel has no horns, but the elephant has tusks as formidable as offensive weapons. Sexual selection could not have caused it, for an animal's beauty or attractiveness is not increased by having four stomachs. It was not that an animal could not live on vegetable substances except with this formation: in a wild state, the food of the ox and of the horse differs but very little, neither does that of the camel and elephant. But, even if the power of chewing the cud gave its possessor such an advantage over other animals, how is it that it has not been universally transmitted to all graminivorous animals? It appears to us that the order Ruminantia offers an insuperable objection to the Evolution theory, except upon the principle that nothing is impossible.

We have endeavoured to show that the true instinct of animals is not derived one from the other, and that man does not possess it in the slightest degree, and that this instinct is replaced in man's mind by reason, from which it differs in every respect. Whilst instinct is perfect at once, and is independent of teaching and of experience, reason is a blank without culture; and therefore, whilst instinct is precisely the same in every species, the reason of the human mind varies in almost every individual according to the amount of culture the mind receives, and in this it differs entirely from the so-called reason of the brutes, which can never be expanded beyond a certain point. The reason of animals is a certain intelligence gained by memory and by experience, which makes them capable of a certain amount of teaching, and the intelligence thus gained is frequently transmitted to their offspring, as in the case of certain dogs, who inherit the faculty of pointing at, springing, and retrieving game, which young pointers, spaniels, and retrievers have been known to do without any instruction. Man does not inherit any substantial faculties; however clever the father, the young child's mind is a blank at birth. We believe, then, that what is called reason in an animal is a totally different sense from the Divine faculty of reason in man, not only in degree, but in kind.

We know that there are certain sensations, such as hunger, thirst, love, anger, likes, dislikes, revenge, memory, fatigue, the sexual passions, and some others which affect man as they do animals, to which may be added cunning; and a kind of consciousness, such as that certain acts will involve punishment, though this belongs rather to memory and experience that such acts have before led to such consequences, but which is totally distinct from the moral consciousness of doing wrong because it is wrong; but the possession of these common sensations does not debar there being a fundamental difference between the mental faculties of man and of animals. Mr. Darwin admits that there is "a great break in the organic chain between man and his nearest allies, which cannot be bridged over by any extinct or living species," which we are called upon to suppose might be filled up by the fossil remains of animals, if we could find them; but the break in the mental faculties between man and the ape is far, far greater, and cannot be bridged over by any amount of fossil remains, nor can analogy to it; for although an ape may have a much more highly-organized structure than an ant, there is nothing to show that the ape is superior to that insect, either in instinct or in intelligence, as displayed in the manner in which an ant, if incapable of removing an object by its own powers, will fetch other ants, until their united efforts are sufficient for the purpose; and if they do not keep aphides to supply them with food, they make predatory excursions to capture slaves to work for them. Do any acts performed by apes exceed these actions of the ant? If, then, neither the instinct nor intelligence of animals has advanced with their organization, why are we to admit that there has been a gradual development from the mind of an ape into that of man, if, as has been shown, all proofs are wanting, and that the missing links in the chain exist only in imagination ?

But when we come to man's moral sense or conscience, the difference is still more striking, though it can be only shortly alluded to here. But as Mr. Darwin admits that there was a time in the gradually ascending organic scale when man or some one of his progenitors was not possessed of an immortal soul, on which the moral sense or conscience, in the true acceptation of the term, is dependent; we cannot see how the sensations, feelings, or instincts not so endowed, could develop into those other feelings and senses which belong, and belong only, to an immortal being. There is all the difference between them, of darkness and light.

There may exist outward similarity with fundamental differences. A wig composed of human hair has every outward similarity to the hair on a human head, but it has the fundamental difference of having no roots, no life,—the outward show, but not the spirit. False teeth have all the outward appearance of real teeth, which, indeed, they generally are, but from which they fundamentally differ in having no real connection with the human frame; they perform the same duties as the living teeth, but the vital principle is wanting. So man may resemble animals in his structure; he may have some sensations and feelings in common with them, but the vital principle, the immortal soul, is present only with man, and presents a gulf that cannot be bridged over, a fundamental difference in kind, and not only in degree.

Mr. Darwin, having declared that there is a much wider interval in mental power between the lowest fishes and the higher apes than between an ape and man,—but which we have endeavoured to show is not the case,—proceeds: " Nor is the difference slight in moral disposition between a barbarian, such as the man described by the old navigator Byron, who dashed his child on the rocks for dropping a basket of sea-urchins, and a Howard or Clarkson ; and in intellect, between a savage who does not use any abstract terms, and a Newton or Shakespeare. Differences of this kind between the highest men of the highest races and the lowest savages, are connected by the finest gradations. Therefore it is possible that they might pass and be developed into each other" (vol. i. p. 35).

In the first place, it is not necessary to go to the antipodes to find such a savage as Byron describes. A visit to the Police-courts of one of the first cities in the civilised world would show us savages who throw their wives over bridges into a river, who thrust them under drays, who knock them down and fracture their skulls, with as little remorse and for as slight provocation, as dropping a basket of sea-urchins, and yet the barbarians who performed these acts are supposed to be of the same race as a Howard or Clarkson.

And, secondly, when it is said that the intellect of such a savage is connected by the finest gradations with the mind of a Newton, and that it is *possible* that they might pass into each other; considering the latitude that has been given to the word " possible " in the ' Descent of Man,' that is not admitting much ; but we are not aware that there is anything to show these " fine gradations," or that much imagination is required to admit the possibility of the mind of a savage developing into that of a highly intellectual man.

We believe the mistake that has been made in comparing the mind of a savage with that of civilised man to be, that the comparison has been with adults of the two races, one of whom has been subjected to culture and education and all the accessories of civilised life

F

from his birth, whilst the other's mind has had no culture and no external civilising influences. To form a correct comparison the cases should be reversed, by placing the new-born child of a highly-intellectual man amongst the rudest savages, and by bringing up the child of a savage with all the care, culture, and surroundings of intellectual life ; then, at the age of thirty or forty, compare the intellectual faculties and moral sense of the two adults, and see how far the normal minds of the two beings really differed, and how much is due to education and surrounding influences. The minds of all men, whether civilised or savage, are at their birth a blank, more or less, but are endowed with an inward power or spirit, of greater or less intensity, which enables them, under culture, like a virgin soil, to produce the richest fruits, but which, if left to themselves, will, like the same soil, bear nothing but weeds or the rankest vegetation.

We have known the children of African savages, of pure negro blood, to have been educated into men of considerable intellectual powers, to have become missionaries, and to have been admitted into holy orders, and to take their places in society. We have ourselves seen the children of the wildest tribes,—totally uncivilised, grossly ignorant, whose hands were against every man and every man's hand against them ;—we have seen these children in school, learning to read and write, and not much, if any, more backward than other children of the same age, and growing up into good, useful, peaceable citizens. If these changes can be produced in the minds of children of savages in one or two generations, why are insensible gradations or myriads of years supposed to be necessary to develop the mind of a savage into that of civilised man ?

We know it may be said that these savages have had

all the benefits of the culture of the highest intellects ; but, when all were savages, how was this high intellect attained ? We do not believe—and all proof is wanting to show—that all men were always savages, or that an interminable time was required to convert an intellectual man into a savage; in the same way that one or two, or a few, generations are sufficient to raise the mind of a savage to that of civilised man, so, only a few, probably fewer, generations would be necessary to degrade the mind of the child of an intellectual man into that of a savage. This, according to Mr. Darwin, " is to take a pitiably low view of human nature," but it is more consonant with common sense and known facts, than to suppose that all men are descended from an African ape.

The human intellect is the free gift of God, and may, to the first created beings, have been given to a greater or less extent. It may have improved in some cases and at various times, and become degraded in others ; but it has not arisen by insensible gradations from the sensations of the lower animals. In all ages God has gifted certain individuals with superior mental powers. Newton, the son of a man of good family, but a farmer, or one who farmed his own land, and who was probably a man of ordinary capacity, could not have inherited his wonderful intellect; he could not have obtained his knowledge from the experience of others, for he struck out new ideas, and established new principles; so that there can be no doubt but that his great mental powers were the gift of that munificent Being " from whom cometh every good and perfect gift." So that Newton did more in one lifetime to advance science and general knowledge than had been done by others during centuries. The same with Shakespeare, Watt, and others in our own time and country, and great men in other

F 2

countries and in other times who have given a sudden advance to literature, science, or art; so that the work of centuries in the chain of mental faculties has been bridged over in the lifetime of one man.

We have endeavoured, as well as our space would admit of, to show that the Darwinian theory, in its full extent, is entirely opposed to the revealed Word of God, and that it will not bear a scientific analysis. We are well aware how many arguments we have omitted, and how much more might be said, and much better said, on the subject; but we hope we have done sufficient to show that the conclusions arrived at in the 'Descent of Man' are too loosely put together, depend too much upon assumptions, upon conjecture, and upon probabilities, not to say possibilities; that there are too many breaks in the chain of evidence, the missing links forming by far the greater proportion; and that the theory is altogether too wanting in all the elements necessary for true philosophical induction, to be deserving of acceptance in a scientific point of view; whilst the extreme boldness and confidence with which the most startling dogmas are put forth by an author standing in such high repute in the scientific world,— the apparent candour, and the manner in which the most unscriptural conclusions are kept in the background, together with the charm of the style, all tend to make the book very dangerous, particularly in the present days of growing scepticism; and we shall not be deterred from expressing our belief in the mischievous results of such opinions passing unchallenged, from any dread of being told that our fears are but the phantoms of an over sensitive imagination.

R. E. PEACH, BRIDGE STREET, BATH.

www.ingramcontent.com/pod-product-compliance
Lightning Source LLC
Chambersburg PA
CBHW081519040426
42447CB00013B/3276